The
WESTERN
KITCHEN

SEASONAL RECIPES FROM
MONTANA'S CHICO HOT SPRINGS RESORT

SEABRING DAVIS

PHOTOGRAPHY BY LYNN DONALDSON-VERMILLION

TWODOT
Guilford, Connecticut
Helena, Montana

A · TWODOT® · BOOK

An imprint of The Rowman & Littlefield Publishing Group, Inc.
4501 Forbes Blvd., Ste. 200
Lanham, MD 20706
www.rowman.com
A registered trademark of The Rowman & Littlefield Publishing Group, Inc.

Distributed by NATIONAL BOOK NETWORK

British Library Cataloguing in Publication Information available

Library of Congress Cataloging-in-Publication Data

Names: Davis, Seabring, author. | Donaldson-Vermillion, Lynn, photographer.
Title: The Western kitchen : seasonal recipes from Montana's Chico Hot
    Springs Resort / written by Seabring Davis ; photography by Lynn
    Donaldson-Vermillion.
Description: Guilford, Connecticut : TwoDot, [2018] | Includes
    bibliographical references and index. |
Identifiers: LCCN 2018006244 (print) | LCCN 2018011518 (ebook) | ISBN
    9781493034383 (e-book) | ISBN 9781493034376 (hardback : alk. paper)
Subjects: LCSH: Cooking, American—Western style. | Cooking—Montana. | Chico
    Hot Springs Resort. | LCGFT: Cookbooks.
Classification: LCC TX715.2.W47 (ebook) | LCC TX715.2.W47 D39 2018 (print) |
    DDC 641.59786—dc23
LC record available at https://lccn.loc.gov/2018006244

♾™ The paper used in this publication meets the minimum requirements of American National Standard for Information Sciences—Permanence of Paper for Printed Library Materials, ANSI/NISO Z39.48-1992.

Printed in the United States of America

This book is dedicated to Colin Kurth Davis,
my partner in love, life, and business.
His passion for wine, great food, and a never-ending party
is infectious, endearing, and admirable.
And to our daughters, Isabel and Simone, who are the best food critics.

Acknowledgments

THIS BOOK WOULD NOT HAVE BEEN POSSIBLE without the encouragement of editor Erin Turner. She is a devoted Chico Hot Springs fan, but also a person who knows what's real. Thank you for recognizing the authentic qualities that Chico still offers to people and for allowing me to have such creative involvement in the process of composing this recipe book.

To Chef Dave Wells, who worked through the busiest season to concoct recipes and who helped elevate every dish. Thank you to the remarkable team in the Chico kitchen, night and day.

To head gardener Jeannie Duran and the super-gardeners, for bringing the most beautiful flowers, fruits, and vegetables to bounty every season.

Thank you to the talented Lynn Donaldson-Vermillion, whose images make the recipes and Chico's culture come to life.

A special thanks to the many friends who helped showcase the human element and fun of Chico Hot Springs: Andrew Doolittle, Brad Kaufman, Ryan and Alexis Whitford, Heidi Saile, Brad Havertape, Matt Jackson, Montana Rose, Katherine and George Borneman, Amy Coolidge, Emma Hewey, Gigi Albiers and her gorgeous family, Alexandra Samy and her tribe for fringe and fun at the Block Party, ER Young in the Saloon, Shane Kehoe and the fabulous night crew in the dining room, Dan Vermillion, Erin Young, Brian O'Connor, Beth and John Gregory, Bryant Bowen and the beautiful brunch team, Tracy Wein, and James Bryant; and behind the scenes, thank you to Machele Shifley, Beth Boston, Joe Engstrom, Doug Wilson, Raymond Buracha and the housekeeping team, and to Sharon Nardin for all the help resurrecting recipes!

To Mike Art for "Hot Wada" and the heart that it took to see the potential in this place so many years ago. Rest in peace.

Finally, this book is for all the employees at Chico, past, present, and future. Thank you for carrying on the story of this place in all that you do.

Contents

Preface

THE BEST MEALS COME WITH A STORY. Whether it's a PBJ-sandwich picnic on a mountain trail or oysters on the half shell at the top of the Eiffel Tower, the story behind a meal is what makes it memorable. The food, of course, should be of good quality, but in reality it is the time and place, and the company we choose to share a bite with, that create the best meals.

Chico Hot Springs is a destination that is brimming with stories.

Established in 1900, it is grounded in pioneer history. Situated in a crag of Paradise Valley at the toe of 10,900-foot Emigrant Peak, it is riddled with tales of adventure, from the Native tribes who migrated through the greater Yellowstone region to the settlers who made their lives in this wild country. Close to Yellowstone National Park, the fabled Yellowstone River,

and the quirky town of Livingston and surrounded by mountain ranges that stretch across Montana and Wyoming, Chico is a place where memories are cemented into our hearts. It holds the traditions of newlyweds, dedicated hot springs fanatics, cowboys, celebrities, and the lore of multigenerational gatherings. It is a place that feels a lot like home, but remains a world apart from everyday stresses.

Particularly in the last forty years, Chico has also become known for its fantastic food. In the historic dining room, it is a priority to serve only the highest-quality meats. The seafood is flown in fresh several times a week. Everything on the menu is made from scratch, and there are hot springs—heated geothermal greenhouses to supply the freshest greens for many months of the year. Yet I would argue that what gets served on each plate is only as good as the company sitting around the table.

In the winter of 1995, my husband, Colin Davis, became the general manager at Chico, and I worked as a waitress in the restaurant. Our Chico story began that year on Christmas Eve. The hotel was full, and the dining room was booked with dinner reservations. Outside, feather-size snowflakes poured from the sky. Paradise Valley old-timers said this was the harshest winter in twenty years.

But inside, the dining room was warm with candlelight, and rustic barn-wood walls wrapped guests and employees in cozy bliss. Every seat in the restaurant was full. There was the clink of wine glasses, the polite clatter of silverware, hushed conversation with an occasional lively outburst of laughter. Couples mooned at tables set for two. A large family group anchored the center of the long room. Most of the diners were hotel guests.

"Our family has celebrated Christmas at Chico for four generations," said a rosy-cheeked woman at the big table. She glanced around the group, pointing out her parents, children, and grandchildren with pride. They were from Billings, a town more than one hundred miles east of the resort. They'd been visiting since the 1950s. Hearing nostalgic memories about Chico's hold on so many guests is an essential part of what makes an experience here a treasure.

From the moment our family purchased the restaurant and resort in 2015, we felt that we were not becoming owners, but caretakers of history, of traditions, and keepers of memories. We feel a kindred responsibility to everyone who carries a story of Chico—whether those who have just discovered Montana or who have lived here all their lives, or young lovers who were married on the front lawn and returned to celebrate anniversaries, birthdays, and holidays with meals shared between friends and family. There are generations of stories like these that add to the rich history of Chico Hot Springs.

On that Christmas Eve many years ago, the snow kept falling outside. The dinner service flowed as I served hard-to-find wines and celebratory bottles of champagne. Plates of robust food—beef Wellington, Grand Marnier duck, and FedEx-delivered fresh king salmon—and the showy flaming orange dessert—rolled out from the kitchen to the pleasure of the guests while the snow piled higher.

New guests stood at the threshold of the heavy barnwood doors, waiting to be seated for dinner, brushing snow off winter jackets. "It's really coming down outside," they'd gush as the host hung their coats and led them to a well-set table.

Once they sat down, they forgot about winter, ensconced in the warmth of the room. As they dined, the blizzard reached extremes. The weight of so many inches of snow pulled down power lines, and we had a blackout at Chico. The snowplows couldn't get through and the roads were closed. We were all snowed in. Everyone who wasn't a registered hotel guest was invited to stay for the night. We stoked the fireplace, handed out flashlights and extra blankets, lit candles, and wished each other Merry Christmas.

In the morning, with the electricity restored and the sky a gleaming blue, the whole resort, its green-and-white clapboard hotel and rustic cabins, was blanketed in white. The natural hot springs huffed steam in dreamy puffs. A mammoth snowplow finally hunkered up the long road, clearing it for travelers. It was the epitome of a winter wonderland that I will always remember.

Today, on any given night the restaurant is full—during the dead of winter, bloom of spring, hottest summer night, or shortest autumn evening. It doesn't matter that the place is a little out of the way—people find it and keep coming back. People drive hundreds of miles to enjoy a meal and a soak at this iconic Montana retreat.

"For over a century Chico Hot Springs has become a ritual for so many people," Colin says. "It's their place, and we always try to remember that the resort is for locals who come back time after time as much as it is for out-of-state visitors who only experience it once."

Through the last two decades, Chico has wrapped our family into the subtext of its mythology. Colin has created a business culture that values service and family and guests. He has restored buildings, cultivated a wine list and restaurant that is unparalleled in the state, expanded the property, and built on a foundation of a place that is special to so many people. Together we have raised two girls on this ground, dined next to Hollywood stars and writers, been dropped mid-dip by a cowboy on the saloon dance floor, dipped our daughters in the hot springs in every season of the year and watched them find Easter eggs on the lawn, shared many meals with people we love, worked closely with the chefs to compile a cookbook, and have cooked arguably all of those classic recipes in our home. Those are our stories. Chico is our story.

But what I love most about the place are the people who return again and again. It's changed, folks say, but then they remember that it has also stayed the same. The locals still say that for one of the best meals in the state, you must go to Chico Hot Springs. It's a Montana tradition.

Seabring and Colin

Introduction: *The Western Kitchen*

COOKING IN THE WESTERN UNITED STATES today means cooking with fresh, regional, local, and high-caliber seasonal ingredients. It's about implementing techniques that bring out authentic tastes: Grill. Smoke. Sous Vide. Brine. Roast. Poach. Sauté. Fry. Bake.

The seasonally inspired recipes in this book apply all of these methods and, when done well, will result in memorable morsels that look as good as they taste.

These days anything can be overnighted to just about anywhere, but at Chico we try to stay true to mountain cuisine, relying on the freshest ingredients to make every dish from scratch. We find the best meats and trout from local Montana farms and ranches. Our culinary team develops relationships with fresh seafood purveyors on both the West and East Coasts, the slightly zany wild mushroom pickers who knock at the back door of the kitchen, and the neighboring ranchers and tireless farmers. Yet the most important source is in our backyard, where two geothermal greenhouses provide the freshest produce available for half the year. The natural runoff from the hot springs flow into our garden's watering system to heat the soil and create a microclimate that extends the high country growing season to begin in early May and end in late October.

The result is that Chico's executive chef, David Wells, eats flowers. He tastes every edible flower—from tiny coriander buds to mustard green sprigs—grown in the garden. He works closely with head gardener Jeannie Duran, from planting to harvesting, to add beautiful and creative elements to the menu offerings. Chef Wells and the Chico team of cooks strive to use every part of the vegetable and any part of the animal, from nose to tail, as ingredients for the delicious recipes they create in the main kitchen. Flavor is the origin of every dish, and it starts with the smallest element.

Long before Chef Wells, the inspiration for this end-of-the-road haven in Montana's gorgeous Paradise Valley came from an unassuming pioneer woman who boldly opened the doors of what was first dubbed the Chico Warm Springs Hotel in 1900. She bought the land for $1 and promised a fresh strawberry with every meal to each of the boarders. Today, it is much easier to come by those strawberries, but our promise at Chico Hot Springs is still to cook food that is fresh and delicious, to offer it with great service, and to welcome our guests back again and again.

Like so many places in the American West, Chico Hot Springs is a blend of old and new, both on the property and in the kitchen. The dinner menu is rooted in European classics, such as beef Wellington and duck confit, but it is also punctuated by modern techniques and multicultural flavors that combine as offerings that could be classified as New American cuisine. Bringing new culinary techniques, such as sous vide—a slow, low-temperature method of cooking—to ensure consistently cooked pork chops or local grass-fed New York steaks adds a contemporary twist to the old image of "meat 'n' potatoes."

If anything, cooking in a Western Kitchen is about serving food that is approachable and scrumptious. It should be easy to eat. It should taste good. That's the foundation for our style of cuisine. Chico is a place that isn't driven by a celebrity chef or a single personality; instead, it's a place where Montana's beauty, history, and spirit come together at this end-of-the-road hotel, where we also happen to serve delicious meals.

At Chico our motto is: *Turn guests into friends and friends into family.* Everyone who cooks in our kitchen is a member of our big family. We hope that you can taste the spirit of family and friends with each recipe in this book. Get cooking!

Note: Recipes with the wagon wheel logo are Chico "Classics."

A Montana Icon: *A Brief History of Chico Hot Springs*

PEOPLE BEGAN RAVING ABOUT THE RESTAURANT at Chico Hot Springs Resort more than a century ago when Percie (Matheson) Knowles and her husband, William E. Knowles, opened its doors at the height of Montana's gold rush. It was a modest Victorian-style boardinghouse that catered to fortune-seekers who mined claims up the road in Emigrant Gulch. Tired from the challenges of hardrock mining, sleeping in tents, eating campfire meals, and washing their "dirty duds" in the creek, the men sought the refinement of what was first known as the Chico Warm Springs Hotel. They were promised a clean bed, hot bath, and fresh strawberries with every meal for a fee of only six dollars a week.

On June 20, 1900, the hotel's grand opening included a brass band, a grand ball, and a Victorian tea. The Knowleses quickly learned that people will travel far for a good soak and a fine meal. A horse-drawn carriage shuttled guests the three miles from the Emigrant train stop to the hotel. Word spread, and Chico quickly became a destination for travelers from Livingston and en route to Yellowstone National Park via the Northern Pacific Railway Park Branch Line. Their business grew from ten rooms to twenty in the span of just a few years. Eventually, the lovely two-story clapboard building boasted a full-service dining room with white linen tablecloths and fine china. A swim in the forty-foot-long, six-foot-deep covered hot springs "plunge" cost just ten cents. Bill and Percie also offered entertainment, including dancing and games on the broad front lawn.

As business boomed, the couple added more rooms and by 1909 offered accommodations for up to sixty guests. Mrs. Knowles became known for her refinement, excellent cooking, and fastidious manner. She had been a teacher who came West to work at the one-room schoolhouse at Old Chico. She was a prohibitionist and a suffragette. By contrast, Bill gained a reputation as a friendly and boisterous host. He built a dance hall on the hill above the hotel and turned a blind eye to rumrunners and teetotalers alike. All were welcome at Chico!

The Knowleses were notoriously at odds with each other about how Chico should be developed. Percie had a vision of creating a state-of-the-art health spa and hospital, touting the curative powers of the natural minerals in the geo-thermal springs. She procured the services of a doctor who practiced at the hotel for several years. But Bill saw better (and livelier) prospects in the dance hall and someday in a full-service saloon. He also pursued sheep ranching. Despite the disparity in their business plans, they managed to find common ground as innkeepers, blending Victorian sophistication with cowboy practicality. Their son, Radbourne, was raised at the

Percie (Matheson) Knowles traveled to Montana from Ontario when she was in her 20s. She joined her sister in 1888 to live with her in the gold mining town of Chico and to teach at the school house. She inherited land with the hot springs from her uncle and paid $1 in taxes to seal her claim to it.

William E. Knowles (front left with knife) and his wife Percie Knowles (fourth woman in center row) opened the doors of Chico Warm Springs Hotel in 1900 as a boarding house for gold miners from nearby Emigrant Gulch.

hotel, and the two balanced the demands of family and business.

In April 1910 Bill Knowles tragically died of liver cirrhosis, and Percie decided to pursue her original dream. By 1912 she stopped serving alcohol on the property. By June of that year, she procured the reputable services of Dr. George A. Townsend as the spa doctor. The good doctor promoted the restorative elements of the mineral pools, vouching for the healing waters as a cure for rheumatism, kidney disease, skin problems, and other internal ailments. He treated patients with symptoms as innocuous as the common cold and as complicated as brain surgery. The latter drew positive recognition throughout the state and as far as North Dakota, Minnesota, and some eastern states.

By 1914 Dr. Townsend's services merited a new addition at Chico: a new twenty-room hospital wing was built onto the northeastern end of the hotel. The build-ing accommodated twenty-four patients and included a lab, an operating room, and six examination rooms. Dr. Townsend practiced at Chico until 1925, when he finally retired and moved near Glacier National Park.

During the 1920s, despite Percie's prim demeanor —and her banishing of alcohol—the dances in the hall

In 1900 the opening of Chico Hot Springs launched with a full brass band and festivities that drew visitors from Bozeman and Billings.

Visitors were greeted with a Chico shuttle at the Emigrant station in the early 1900s.

til midnight. Guests were encouraged to stay overnight, hunt game on the vast acreage, and fish in the trout pond. A five-acre garden serviced the needs of guests who dined at Chico, and a row of deluxe tents were set up behind the main building to accommodate the overflow. These were high times for Chico Hot Springs.

Following Dr. Townsend's retirement, Chico became more health spa than hospital. Several doctors took up residence at the hotel through the decades. As time passed, the mining activity faded, Paradise Valley remained a thoroughfare for Yellowstone travelers, and ranching remained an economic mainstay. As Percie Knowles aged, she was worn down by the demands of the large property. With the Great Depression and throughout the 1930s, visitation to the hotel and the natatorium flagged. Many of the rooms were closed and taken out of commission. Ultimately, Percie succumbed to mental illness and was sent to the state hospital, where she eventually passed away in 1941.

In Percie's absence, her son and his wife, Sophia, took over the property with the help of several dedicated

on the hill continued. Old-timers still remember the stories about the crowds overflowing from the dance hall. Dr. Townsend's retirement party was rumored to have hosted five hundred people in the dance hall and a "turkey supper" served in the hotel dining room un-

Head gardener Bill Tolbet holds a massive cabbage in the 5-acre gardens that he tended at Chico for the 10 years he worked with the Knowles family.

William E. Knowles, Chico's first proprietor, is pictured on the far left after a successful duck hunt with friends. He was a gold miner, sheep and cattle rancher and widely known as a generous host who welcomed guests to the hot springs with gregarious stories of the hunting and fishing in the area which he touted as "the best in the world."

Radbourne Campbell Knowles, the only child of Bill and Percie, was born January 13, 1898. He grew up on the grounds of Chico Hot Springs and later attended private schools, served in the Army during WW I, then attended the agricultural college in Bozeman. After college, Radbourne wed Agnes Sophia Blegenzahn, who had come from North Dakota to work at Chico in 1917. The couple married in 1919 and eventually ran the resort until the 1940s. After Radbourne's death, his war buddy Eddy Leak, who was an entertainer and handyman on the property, helped Sophia Knowles run the hotel until it was sold years later.

longtime employees and family friends. But Radbourne Knowles didn't have the same passion to be a hotelier as his mother did, and under his leadership business was dismal. He suffered from injuries incurred during his service in World War I and died in 1943. Sophia continued to oversee Chico until 1948, when she sold it to Oneita "Nita" Benke. The addition of a saloon was Nita's biggest contribution to the business. As proprietress she hosted the Mel Bay Dance Group for a week each year and offered lively dancing events.

Nita rebuilt the business at Chico Hot Springs Hotel with her first husband, Joe Davis, by marketing it to tour groups with the Northern Pacific Railroad as well as local hunting and fishing guides. Joe Davis passed away in 1950 and later Nita married John Broderick. Together the couple cultivated customers who were interested in a western experience that featured horseback riding, hunting and fishing forays, and chuck-wagon cookouts. They held weekly rodeos, and eventually the business became the Chico Ranch.

The Brodericks brought all the flair of a traditional dude ranch to their conversion of Chico from a hospital to a resort. Their renovated dining room seated 110 people, attracting large groups from as far as San Fran-

cisco and New York City to visit Chico Hot Springs as an annual tradition.

Eventually the Brodericks retired to a private ranch life and sold the business to Julian and Alma Read. After the Reads, ownership shifted several times in the mid-twentieth century. The Reads sold Chico to John Sterhan and his family, and a few years later, Jake Franks bought it from the Sterhans. The property, then known as Chico Ranch and Lodge, went through a lot of transition in the 1950s and 1960s. The roof over the plunge pool collapsed, and the owners turned it into an open-air pool with a carpeted deck. The saloon limped along, but the restaurant was barely open. Gradually the whole property fell into disrepair.

In 1973 Mike and Eve Art, of Cleveland, Ohio, bought the rundown property with partners Don Conway and Bob Jackson. By 1976 the Arts had moved to Montana with their young daughters, Andie and Jackie, in tow to begin a dream life in Big Sky Country. Eve—in good humor and with fond memories—later called what they had walked into "a disaster." Chico was a sad and neglected western hotel.

Still, the Art family dove into their new role as Montana innkeepers. Bit by bit, they improved the property,

Preparing the 1906 dining room for dinner service, Molly Dorgan, Mabel Freeland, and Frieda Frick set the tables.

In January, 1908, famous Western artist Charlie Russell visited Chico. Pictured from left to right: Bill "Buck" Buchanan, John Matheson, Charles M. Russell, and Bill Deeton at Chico Hot Springs, Montana.

In 1909 cheeky employees in the "snack bar" sold cigars and other tobacco products on one side and sodas and candy on the other.

In 1912 three bathing beauties in customary swimming "suits" enjoyed the two large hot springs pools.

Posing in glamorous housekeeping uniforms, Betsy Jacobsen, Bertha Mikkelson, Elsie Aarestad, Ida LaRue and her sister, worked at Chico waiting tables and housekeeping in 1915.

fixing leaks in the roofs, replacing heating systems, and adding "modern" lodging with the help of many neighbors. Their efforts resulted in a listing on the National Register of Historic Places for the main hotel. But by far the most significant change that the Art family conceived was the idea of creating a fine-dining restaurant that would attract a discerning clientele. They brought in Chef Larry Edwards and started serving elegant dinners with tableside service and a tremendous wine list.

Word of the delicious food spread, and Chico Hot Springs Resort blossomed from a tired hotel with only three employees to a popular destination during the 1980s and early 1990s. The Arts became widely known for their hospitality and generosity. They built friend-

The freedom of automobile travel increased visitors to Chico Hot Springs for the health spa and hotel from 1915 onward.

As more guests discovered the hotel at Chico Hot Springs, the Knowles erected a row of tents behind the hospital wing in 1915, the original "glamping."

ships with locals and visiting guests who sought out this quirky, end-of-the-road place.

After owning the resort for over four decades, the Art family sold their wonderful business to their partner of twenty years, Colin Davis, in 2015. Mike Art passed away in 2017; he will always be remembered at Chico.

Today Colin Davis carries on the legacy that he helped build alongside the Art family. He generated major changes since taking a role at Chico in 1995, including the construction of a modern convention center and wedding facility; the addition of luxury cabins, a customized sleeping caboose, and a Conestoga wagon Cowboy Camp;

Multiple swings on the front lawn of the hotel were favorite activities for children and families in 1918.

In 1919 an addition and new dormers were added to the original Chico Hot Springs Hotel. The front lawn was used for games and gatherings.

John and Nita Broderick were the second owners of Chico and changed it from a "health resort and hospital" to a ranch in 1948 where guests enjoyed horseback riding, guided fishing and hunting trips, as well as a lively saloon with dancing again.

By the 1960s, Chico had changed owners several times and showed signs of wear. The hospital wing on the left was torn down in the 1930s and replaced with a shed-style roofed building that housed the former convention hall.

In 1968 the dilapidated Chico Hot Springs Resort shows the property after the natatorium roof collapsed and was replaced with an open-air pool.

Alma and Julian Read purchased "Chico Ranch" in 1964.

The Sterhan family gathered in the hotel lobby in 1968 for this photo during the tenure when Susie and John raised their children, Dorrie, Sandy, Freddie, and Donny as the owners of Chico between 1967 to 1972.

Jake and Myra Franks briefly owned Chico Ranch with the Britt family (Barbara and Gary, with children Rodney and Lori) for a year and a half.

As the resort evolved to become a guest ranch, during the 1970s the lobby became a casual lounge for guests.

Mike and Eve Art rescued Chico Hot Springs from its dilapidated state in 1973 and owned the property until 2015.

the reclamation of an extensive garden; and the creation of mountain biking trails, and has overseen the growth of one of Montana's most beloved getaways. With his wife, Seabring Davis, and two daughters, Isabel and Simone, he continues to build on that enterprising dream that started in 1900. The restaurant continues to be the hub of the resort, proving after so many decades that people really will travel great distances for a fine meal.

For over a century Chico Hot Springs has been hosting parties and entertaining guests from all over the world, whether they are cowhands or celebrities.

What makes this rustic resort unique is its history and ambience. The combination of culinary expertise, a chef's garden and greenhouse, regional ingredients, and the subtle elegance of Chico Hot Springs brings people together to share celebrations, festive gatherings, traditions, and simple meals. Through the decades it has remained an independent family business; it is one of the state's oldest continually operating businesses and has affectionately become known to locals as "Montana's backyard."

Brunch

SUNDAY BRUNCH AT CHICO is a weekend tradition. It starts with a little journey driving through Paradise Valley, preferably on old East River Road as it winds past small country schools, windmills, and black Angus cows that stand like sculptures in fields that roll up to the feet of the Absaroka Mountains. Turn onto the county road to Chico and Emigrant Peak. Inside the historic hotel, nestle into the cozy dining room and begin the meal with a refreshing mimosa, then indulge in the lavish buffet. Quiches, Citrus Salmon, thick and crispy bacon, cheesecakes, Cinnamon Bread Pudding, half a dozen different pastries, and an omelet bar are just a few of the items offered. Afterward, soak in the hot springs pool to complete the leisurely morning, with perhaps just one more mimosa poolside.

Note: Recipes denoted by are Chico "Classics."

Cinnamon Bread Pudding ☾
with Vanilla Bourbon Sauce

This is a true comfort-food dessert. Baking it will fill your house with the warm, welcoming aromas of brown sugar, cinnamon, and vanilla. You can use any kind of bread or pastry—yesterday's French bread, doughnuts, cinnamon rolls, cake crumbs. But consider the occasion, because it will be a more refined dish if you use the same kind of bread for the whole dish.

SERVES 12

Ingredients

FOR THE CINNAMON BREAD PUDDING:

1 cup firmly packed brown sugar

10 cups chopped day-old bread or pastry

3 cups half-and-half

2 cups heavy whipping cream

½ cup granulated sugar

5 eggs

1 tablespoon cinnamon

FOR THE VANILLA BOURBON SAUCE:

2 cups heavy whipping cream

1 cup firmly packed brown sugar

1 tablespoon pure vanilla extract

¼ teaspoon cinnamon

1 tablespoon bourbon (can also substitute brandy or orange liqueur)

Instructions

TO PREPARE THE CINNAMON BREAD PUDDING:

Mix all ingredients in a large bowl; let soak for 20 minutes, stirring occasionally.

Preheat oven to 350°F. Spray a 9 x 13-inch baking dish with cooking spray. Spray a piece of aluminum foil to use for covering later.

Pour bread pudding mixture into the baking pan. Cover with foil and bake for 1 hour, or until center of pudding is firm. The bread pudding can be made 1 or 2 days in advance; reheat at 250°F for about 30 minutes before serving.

TO PREPARE THE VANILLA BOURBON SAUCE:

Pour heavy cream into a saucepan and bring to a gentle boil over medium heat. Continue to boil until cream is reduced by almost half, about 30 minutes. Be careful to stir periodically to keep cream from scalding. Add brown sugar, vanilla, cinnamon, and bourbon and allow to boil until sauce thickens slightly, another 15 minutes.

TO SERVE:

Slice into twelve squares in the baking dish, then pour 1 cup of warm sauce over warm bread pudding. Scoop onto plates and drizzle remaining sauce over the top of each pudding square; garnish with whipped cream and berries if desired.

Sour Cream Coffee Cake Muffins

Delicate and dense, this recipe can be divided into muffins or prepared as a cake that produces results that are just as satisfying for dessert as for breakfast. Berries work best with this recipe, but other fruits such as peaches, or even cherries, are lovely, too.

SERVES 12

Ingredients

½ cup (1 stick) unsalted butter, softened and cubed

1 cup granulated sugar

3 eggs

2 cups all-purpose flour

2 teaspoons baking powder

1 teaspoon baking soda

2 cups sour cream

1½ teaspoons pure vanilla extract

1 pint fresh blueberries (or fruit of your choice; thawed, drained frozen fruit can be substituted)

¼ cup powdered sugar, for dusting

Instructions

Preheat oven to 350°F. Spray a medium muffin pan with cooking spray.

Cream butter and sugar in a mixing bowl. Add eggs one at a time, scraping sides and bottom of bowl between additions. Sift flour, baking powder, and baking soda together. Alternately add dry ingredients and sour cream to butter mixture. Add vanilla and combine thoroughly, but do not overmix.

Spoon batter into muffin tins, filling to the halfway point. (If preparing a cake, spread half the batter in a prepared springform pan and follow the remaining instructions on a larger scale.) Place a layer of fruit on top of the batter. Carefully spread remaining batter on top of the fruit, using a metal spatula dipped in hot water to evenly distribute the batter to thoroughly cover the fruit, filling the muffin tin three-quarters of the way to the top to allow for rising. Bake for 25 to 30 minutes (30 to 45 minutes for cake), or until the muffins are firm to the touch; a toothpick inserted should come out clean. Cool completely and remove from pan. Sprinkle with powdered sugar and garnish with remaining fruit.

Montana Snowball Cookies ☀

Brunch at Chico is an extensive meal; dessert is included in the big splurge. Tuck a couple of these sweet treats into your pocket to sneak while you are out dogsledding. They'll take the chill out of the real snow and give you a quick burst of energy so you can keep up with the dogs.

MAKES 3 DOZEN COOKIES

Ingredients

1 cup (2 sticks) unsalted butter

½ cup sifted powdered sugar

1 teaspoon pure vanilla extract

2¼ cups all-purpose flour

¼ teaspoon salt

¼ cup finely chopped pecans

½ cup powdered sugar, for dusting

Instructions

Preheat oven to 350°F.

Cream butter and sugar with an electric mixer until light and fluffy. Add vanilla, flour, salt, and pecans; mix until a loose dough ball forms. Roll into 1-inch balls and place on a baking sheet lined with parchment paper about 2 inches apart. Bake for 10 to 12 minutes. Remove from oven and immediately roll hot cookies in powdered sugar to coat. Let cookies cool and roll in powdered sugar again.

Caramel Pecan Rolls ✺

After an arduous week working on a travel story about Chico Hot Springs, the editorial staff from *Outdoor Life* magazine returned to New York City. Within forty-eight hours of arriving home, the crew bemoaned their life without Chico's caramel rolls. Chico promptly overnighted two dozen rolls. This recipe is that good.

MAKES 1 DOZEN ROLLS

Ingredients

FOR THE DOUGH:

2½ cups plus 2 tablespoons all-purpose flour

6 tablespoons granulated sugar

1 tablespoon instant yeast

½ teaspoon cinnamon

¾ teaspoon salt

¾ cup water

1½ tablespoons unsalted butter

2 tablespoons plus ¼ teaspoon vegetable shortening

1 egg

FOR THE FILLING:

1 cup (2 sticks) unsalted butter, softened

1 cup firmly packed brown sugar

1½ teaspoons cinnamon

FOR THE TOPPING:

1 cup heavy whipping cream

1 cup firmly packed brown sugar

1 cup pecans, rough chopped (optional)

Instructions

TO PREPARE THE DOUGH:

Combine flour, sugar, yeast, cinnamon, and salt in the bowl of an electric mixer or in a large mixing bowl if preparing by hand. In a saucepan heat water, butter, and shortening until it reaches 120° to 130°F. Break egg into a medium bowl. Slowly pour the butter mixture into the egg while whisking. Add this mixture to the dry ingredients in the mixing bowl fitted with a dough hook or use a large metal spoon to mix, adding additional flour to make a soft, workable dough. Place in a greased bowl and cover with plastic wrap. Let the dough rise until doubled in size, about 30 to 45 minutes.

TO PREPARE THE FILLING:

While dough is rising, mix the butter, brown sugar, and cinnamon until it reaches a paste consistency. Set aside.

TO PREPARE THE TOPPING:

Combine cream and brown sugar and whip to a sour cream–like consistency. Cover the bottom of a 9 x 13-inch glass baking dish with topping, sprinkle with pecans to cover, and set aside.

TO ASSEMBLE AND BAKE:

When dough is ready, roll into an 18 x 10-inch rectangle about ½ inch thick. Spread the filling on the dough and roll tightly lengthwise. Cut into 1-inch-thick rolls and place in the glass baking dish; the rolls should be almost touching. Cover the pan with plastic wrap and let rise once more until almost doubled, about 30 minutes.

Shortly before rolls have finished rising, preheat oven to 350°F. Remove the plastic and bake for 25 to 30 minutes, or until topping is golden and clear.

Remove pan from oven and immediately remove rolls by inverting pan onto a serving tray or baking sheet. Pour any excess liquid over the rolls. Let cool slightly and serve warm.

Granola ☕

With milk or yogurt, this house-made granola gives you a hearty start to the day. Made with walnuts, almonds, coconut, and sunflower seeds, this cereal has a healthy dose of protein wrapped up in a sweet maple-honey flavor. Serve it with warm milk on cold winter days for a great alternative to oatmeal.

MAKES 8 CUPS

Ingredients

3 cups rolled oats

1¼ cups bran flakes

¾ cup shredded sweetened coconut

½ cup chopped walnuts

1 cup sliced almonds

¾ cup salted sunflower seeds

2 teaspoons cinnamon

2½ teaspoons pure maple syrup

¾ cup honey

¾ cup canola oil

Instructions

Preheat oven to 350°F. Prepare two baking sheets by covering with wax or parchment paper; grease paper with cooking spray.

Combine oats, bran flakes, coconut, walnuts, almonds, sunflower seeds, and cinnamon in a large bowl. In a separate bowl, mix maple syrup, honey, and oil; add to dry mixture and stir until well combined. Divide the mixture between each prepared cookie sheet; spread evenly. Bake for 20 to 25 minutes until golden brown, tossing granola halfway through the baking time to keep edges from burning. Let cool completely before storing.

Citrus Salmon ☀

Delicious and simple, the tangy marinade offers a perfect balance for the salmon's oily flesh. On any given Sunday you will find this dish offered at Chico's extensive brunch buffet. It is also wonderful for a light dinner. For an extra detail, thinly slice fresh citrus and overlay onto the fish before roasting to create the effect of fish scales.

SERVES 6

Ingredients

Zest and juice of 2 oranges

½ cup chopped fresh parsley

2 tablespoons chopped garlic

Juice of 1 lime

1 cup extra-virgin olive oil

1 (2-pound) Coho salmon fillet, skin on and pin bones removed

Instructions

Preheat oven to 400°F. Grease a roasting pan or baking dish (at least 9 x 13 inches) with cooking spray.

In a bowl, combine orange zest (reserve juice), parsley, garlic, lime juice, and olive oil. Arrange salmon in the prepared pan or dish. Liberally brush on citrus-parsley mixture; let stand 10 minutes. Pour orange juice over the top of fish and bake for 10 minutes. Salmon should be tender and flaky when finished.

Four-Cheese Quiche ☾

This simple, creamy quiche with a light, flaky crust is a brunch staple. It works as a vegetarian option as is or as the ideal palette for a build-your-own version. Try seasonal ingredients from the garden—thinly sliced summer squash or kale add color and flavor to this basic recipe.

SERVES 8

Ingredients

FOR THE CRUST:

2 tablespoons unsalted butter

2 tablespoons shortening

1 cup all-purpose flour

¼ cup milk

FOR THE BATTER:

6 eggs

1 cup heavy whipping cream

½ teaspoon black pepper

½ teaspoon dried mustard

FOR THE FILLING:

½ cup shredded medium-sharp cheddar cheese

½ cup shredded Monterey Jack cheese

½ cup shredded Swiss cheese

½ cup shredded smoked Gouda cheese

Instructions

TO PREPARE THE CRUST:

Preheat oven to 350°F. Grease an 8-inch pie pan with cooking spray.

Combine butter, shortening, and flour. Blend ingredients with a fork until butter and shortening are fully incorporated; the dough will be slightly lumpy. Add milk and mix until ingredients are just wet. Roll out dough on a lightly floured surface and press into prepared pan. Bake for 7 minutes. Set aside. Reduce oven temperature to 300°F.

TO PREPARE THE BATTER:

Mix eggs, cream, black pepper and mustard in a bowl and set aside.

TO PREPARE THE FILLING AND ASSEMBLE:

Combine all cheeses. In the reserved pie crust, add cheese mixture and pour egg batter over the top. Place on a baking sheet to catch overflow during baking. Bake for 30 to 40 minutes, or until quiche is golden brown and firm.

Thai Duck Salad ☾

The succulent duck adds a touch of elegance and richness to this simple salad. It is ideal for a light meal as well as for a dinner salad. Prepare the Thai vinaigrette a day in advance of serving it on this salad.

SERVES 4–6

Ingredients

FOR THE THAI VINAIGRETTE:
Juice of 1 lime

1 tablespoon minced garlic

1 tablespoon brown sugar

2 cups rice wine vinegar

¾ cup extra-virgin olive oil

2 teaspoons sesame oil

1 tablespoon honey

1 tablespoon Tabasco sauce (or less, according to your taste for spice)

FOR THE SALAD:
1 roasted duck (see Duck Grand Marnier Two Ways, recipe page 121)

1 pound mixed greens

1 red pepper, sliced

5 scallions, chopped

¼ cup canned mandarin orange segments, drained

Instructions

TO PREPARE THE THAI VINAIGRETTE:
Mix all ingredients together and let stand overnight.

TO PREPARE THE SALAD:
Remove skin from roasted and cooled duck and shred meat by hand; place in a large bowl. In a separate bowl, combine mixed greens, red pepper, and scallions; add duck meat. Just before serving, add mandarin oranges and toss salad with Thai vinaigrette, coating thoroughly.

Eggplant Timbale ☾

This delicate dish is a wonderful alternative to quiche and considerably easier than a soufflé. The eggs and the sour cream combine to give it a light, creamy texture. It's perfect as a side dish or a special item for an afternoon brunch.

SERVES 8

Ingredients

1 red bell pepper

4 eggs, beaten

¼ cup sour cream

½ cup shredded Monterey Jack cheese

½ cup bread crumbs

2 tablespoons chopped fresh parsley, divided

1 tablespoon canola oil

1 medium yellow onion, diced

2 shallots, diced

2 tablespoons unsalted butter

2 medium eggplants

Instructions

Roast the bell pepper over an open flame on a gas-burning stovetop or grill; remove from flame when skin is mostly blackened and immerse pepper in an ice bath to remove skin easily. Seed and dice. (Pepper can also be roasted in a 400°F oven for 10 to 20 minutes and then peeled.)

In a bowl, mix half of the diced pepper, beaten eggs, sour cream, cheese, bread crumbs, and 1 tablespoon parsley. In a medium-size frying pan, heat canola oil over medium heat, then sauté onion and shallots in butter until sweated. Remove onions and shallots from heat and set aside to cool for approximately 10 minutes. Add to the bowl with bell pepper and egg mixture.

Slice eggplants in 1/4-inch rounds, keeping the skin on and discarding the end pieces. Grill or sauté the eggplant until soft but not mushy (if sautéing, it's okay to reuse the same pan that was used to cook the onions and shallots).

Preheat oven to 350°F. Line the bottom and sides of a well-greased 8-inch custard bowl or terrine mold with slices of cooked eggplant. Be sure to cover all surface area by overlapping eggplant slices (you will have leftover eggplant slices). Place the filling mixure into the eggplant bowl. Top with the remaining eggplant.

Place the eggplant bowl in a separate baking dish filled with hot water; the water should come halfway up the outside of the bowl. Bake for 25 minutes. Press gently on the top of the eggplant to check for readiness; it should feel firm.

Remove from the oven and let stand in the water bath for 10 minutes. To serve, run a knife around the sides of the dish to release the eggplant. Put a large serving plate on top of the timbale and flip it over. Lift the bowl; the timbale should come out easily. Tap the bottom of the bowl if it sticks. Sprinkle the remaining red pepper and parsley on top for garnish.

Salmon Tartare with Crème Fraîche Blinis and Balsamic "Caviar"

To create this elegant classic requires a conscious bit of planning. The crème fraîche is easily purchased at the market, so you might skip that step, but the freshly made blinis are a must to achieve the full effect of this toothsome and slightly citrusy tartare on an air-thin little pancake with a tangy cream sauce and burst of balsamic. Every step is worth the effort.

SERVES 8–10

Ingredients

FOR THE CRÈME FRAÎCHE:

1 cup heavy whipping cream

2 tablespoons whole buttermilk

FOR THE SALMON TARTARE:

12 ounces sushi grade salmon, diced

1 tablespoon olive oil

3 tablespoons fresh lime juice

Sea salt and freshly ground black pepper to taste

FOR THE BLINIS:

½ cup all-purpose flour

½ cup buckwheat flour

4 teaspoons granulated sugar

1¼ teaspoons active dry yeast

¼ teaspoon salt

1 cup whole milk

5 tablespoons unsalted butter, cubed and divided

2 large eggs, beaten

FOR THE BALSAMIC "CAVIAR"

1 cup canola oil (or similar neutral oil)

¾ cup balsamic vinegar

1 scant teaspoon of agar

Instructions

TO PREPARE THE CRÈME FRAÎCHE:

In a glass jar, combine heavy cream and buttermilk. Shake the liquid until combined, then remove the lid. Cover loosely with parchment paper or a coffee filter tied onto the jar with string and let sit overnight (or up to 24 hours) undisturbed and unrefrigerated. For the best results, the temperature in your kitchen should be between 72 and 78°F. It will be thick and creamy when ready, almost as stiff as sour cream, and will keep for 2 weeks in the refrigerator.

TO PREPARE THE SALMON TARTARE:

Toss diced salmon with oil and lime juice. Season the salmon mixture with a little salt and pepper to taste.

TO PREPARE THE BLINIS:

Mix flours, sugar, yeast, and salt together. In a small saucepan over medium-high, heat milk and 3 tablespoons butter to 110°F. Whisk in dry ingredients, cover with plastic wrap, and let rise until doubled in size, about 1 hour. After proofing, whisk in eggs until well incorporated. The batter can be made one day in advance, refrigerated overnight. Whisk the batter before using. To cook the thin pancakes, heat in a nonstick pan to medium, melt a little butter, adding more as needed while making the blinis. Spoon in enough batter to make a pancake about the size of a silver dollar and cook for approximately 1 minute on each side until golden brown. Since these are best served warm, hold them in an oven set to the lowest temperature while cooking the remaining batter. Repeat until all batter is used.

TO PREPARE THE BALSAMIC "CAVIAR":

Place oil in the freezer for an hour. It is important that the oil is very cold because that is what will cause the beads of vinegar to set. Bring balsamic to a boil. Whisk in agar. Using a syringe, drop the balsamic mixture into the oil in small drops. Strain out the pearls of "caviar" and rinse under cold water.

TO ASSEMBLE:

Spoon an ounce of salmon onto each blini and top with crème fraîche and balsamic caviar.

Eggs Benedict with Smoked Duck and Roasted Tomato Hollandaise

Reinventing the blue-chip standard for breakfast is a true Western Kitchen tactic. Here, Chef Dave Wells replaced the common ham with smoked duck and tweaked the classic hollandaise with an additional layer of flavor to create a new take on a delicious favorite.

SERVES 8

Ingredients

FOR THE SMOKED DUCK:

4 duck breasts

½ cup kosher salt

½ cup brown sugar

1 tablespoon canola oil (for searing in the skillet)

FOR THE ROASTED TOMATO PUREE HOLLANDAISE:

1 large Roma tomato

1 tablespoon olive oil

1 tablespoon chopped parsley

4 egg yolks

2 tablespoons lemon juice

1 teaspoon Tabasco

1 cup plus 2 tablespoons melted unsalted butter, warm

Salt to taste

FOR THE EGGS AND MUFFINS:

8 eggs

4 whole English muffins

Instructions

TO PREPARE THE DUCK:

With a sharp knife, score the fat on the duck breasts with three crosshatched slices on the surface. Rub the salt and brown sugar on the breasts. Wrap in plastic wrap and let cure overnight in the refrigerator. Rinse the breasts and pat dry with a towel. Smoke with apple wood at 180°F over a bowl of ice for 1 hour. (See "Cooking Techniques" on page 194 for more information on smoking, but be sure to follow your manufacturer's instructions.)

TO MAKE THE ROASTED TOMATO HOLLANDAISE:

Preheat oven to 400°F. Toss one large Roma tomato with olive oil. Roast in oven until skin is blistered and golden brown, approximately 8 to 10 minutes. Puree tomato in a blender. Set aside to cool.

Put egg yolks, lemon juice, and Tabasco in a food processor. Process until yolks are fluffy. While the processor is still running, slowly drizzle in the warm melted butter until emulsified. If the hollandaise starts getting too thick, it can be thinned by adding a drop or two of warm water. Once emulsified fold in the tomato puree, parsley, and salt to taste.

TO ASSEMBLE:

Slice the duck breast about ¼ inch thick and sear in a skillet with a little canola oil. Poach the eggs. Toast the English muffins—to heat them all at once, place the sliced muffins onto a sheet pan in the oven at 350°F and toast for 5 to 10 minutes. Place poached eggs on muffins. Lay the duck on the eggs and spoon a couple of tablespoons of the hollandaise over the top.

Orchard Apple Pie

crust hard to handle GF

On the hillside next to the Chico garden is a mini fruit orchard. It's an experiment of sorts, with different varieties of apples and plums. The resident deer usually win the bulk of the harvest, but if you act swiftly, just after an early September frost you can pick enough Granny Smiths for a memorable apple pie. It's a little tart, retaining the slightest bit of fresh apple crispness with just the right amount of sweet.

SERVES 8

Ingredients

FOR THE CRUST:

6 ounces cream cheese, room temperature

1 cup (2 sticks) unsalted butter

2½ cups all-purpose flour   *2 c gluten free*

¼ cup milk (to brush on top crust)

FOR THE FILLING:

½ cup (1 stick) unsalted butter

1 cup light brown sugar

2 pounds Granny Smith apples, cored, peeled, and cut into 1-inch-thick slices

1 tablespoon ground cinnamon

½ teaspoon salt

2 tablespoons fresh lemon juice

1 teaspoon pure vanilla extract

2 T Cornstarch

Instructions

TO PREPARE THE CRUST:

In a mixing bowl, cream the cheese and butter until blended, then add the flour all at once. Mix until a dough ball forms. Divide into two balls, flatten, and wrap in plastic wrap. Place in the refrigerator until chilled, about 45 minutes to 1 hour.

TO PREPARE THE FILLING:

Melt butter and sugar in a sauté pan over medium heat. In a bowl, toss apples with cinnamon, salt, lemon juice, and vanilla until thoroughly coated with cinnamon. Add apple mixture to the pan, stirring to combine evenly. Cook until apples are soft when poked with a fork. Remove from heat and let cool.

TO ASSEMBLE AND BAKE:

Preheat oven to 350°F. Remove one dough round from the refrigerator and roll into an 11-inch-diameter circle on a floured surface. Carefully fit into a 9-inch glass pie pan. Moisten edges of bottom crust with water. Fill crust with prepared apple mixture.

Remove remaining dough round from the refrigerator and roll into an 11-inch-diameter circle. Place over top of the filling. Trim edges and gently tuck the top crust under the bottom crust. With your fingers, pinch a decorative edge all the way around the crust. Either create a lattice crust or simply slice a few small vent holes in the top crust with a sharp knife, being careful not to cut through to the bottom crust. Brush top crust with milk and place pie pan on a baking sheet to catch drippings.

Bake the pie for 50 minutes, until crust is golden. Cool slightly on a wire rack to serve warm, or cool completely to serve later. Top with vanilla ice cream or whipped cream.

Chico Plum and Blueberry Cobbler

At the end of August, the plum tree in the Chico garden is heavy with ripe, purple-black fruit. Small but juicy, the abundance of these plums inspires a flurry of jams and cobblers in the short window of ripeness.

SERVES 8

Ingredients

FOR THE COBBLER:

½ cup water

½ cup port or sweet red wine

1½ pounds fresh or frozen blueberries

½ pound Italian plums, pitted

½ cup granulated sugar

1 teaspoon ground cinnamon

2 tablespoons fresh lemon juice

3 tablespoons cornstarch

½ cup water

FOR THE SHORTBREAD:

½ cup (1 stick) unsalted butter, softened

½ cup granulated sugar

1 egg yolk

¾ cup all-purpose flour

½ teaspoon baking powder

Pinch of salt

Instructions

Preheat oven to 350°F.

In a medium-size saucepan, combine water and port or wine. Add berries, plums, sugar, cinnamon, and lemon juice. Stir to combine and bring to a boil over medium heat. Whisk together cornstarch and ½ cup water to make a slurry. Stir into berry mixture and boil to thicken. Remove berries from heat and pour into eight individual ramekins or a 9 x 9-inch glass baking dish.

While berries are cooling, cream together the unsalted butter, sugar, and egg yolk in the bowl of a stand mixer fitted with the paddle attachment. In a separate bowl, whisk together flour, baking powder, and salt. Add flour mixture to the creamed butter and sugar and mix to combine.

Crumble shortbread on top of berry mixture. Bake until shortbread is golden brown and berry mixture is bubbling, about 10 to 12 minutes. Serve with vanilla bean ice cream.

Note: Shortbread dough can be made ahead of time and chilled in the refrigerator for up to two days.

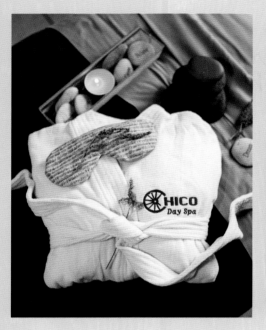

POOLSIDE IN SPRING

THE HOT SPRINGS ARE OPEN ALL YEAR LONG, but a spring pool party is the perfect plan to launch into a new season in Montana. At Chico the pool is a fantastic social scene, unifying the most unlikely guests around the common love of "hot potting," or soaking in geothermally heated water. From babies to bikers, the hot water is an elixir for everyone.

Surrounded by mountains and that big Montana sky, this open-air gathering place is also bookended by the Poolside Grille and our classic Saloon, serving up burgers and fries, beef tenderloin pasties with a flaky crust, and locally brewed beer. The sweet Wagon Wheel sandwiches made with freshly baked chocolate chip cookies and local Wilcoxson's ice cream, so big and gooey that it becomes a race to eat it before the goodness melts, make for an impromptu party by the pool.

There's an art to finding the comfort zone in the pool, the right balance between relaxing warmth and overheating. It takes time. It is a process that can't be rushed, and requires a mindset shift from our busy lives. A good soak can often last for over an hour, moving from the large pool that hovers at 96°F into the smaller pool for a joint-soothing dip in 104°F water and then out onto the side of the deck to cool off. Next, take the plunge and repeat!

Pool Bar
SERVICE WINDOW

Please Be Prepared To Show ID

Please
RING BELL FOR SERVICE

Starters

IF YOU ONLY GET ONE CHANCE to make a first impression, as the saying goes, then these small plates are on the right track. From the classic Fennel Breadsticks, which have been a complimentary offering at Chico since the mid-1970s, to the deconstructed Ahi Wonton with Avocado Slaw and Citrus Chili Aioli, this selection of appetizers captures the diverse flavors of a unique American restaurant. The trout in these recipes is straight from the waters of Paradise Valley, the local chèvre is smoked out back, and the bison is native to these parts. It's the perfect way to begin a meal.

Note: Recipes denoted by are Chico "Classics."

Fennel Breadsticks ☀

These light and crispy breadsticks have been served at the dinner table since 1973. A recipe from Chef Larry Edwards, over the years it has been requested most by guests. The secret to making these at home is to not overmix the dough and to gently roll out the pieces before baking.

MAKES 4 DOZEN BREADSTICKS

Ingredients

½ cup beer, room temperature

½ cup warm water (approximately 110°F)

1½ teaspoons instant yeast

3 cups bread flour

¾ teaspoon salt

½ cup extra-virgin olive oil

3 tablespoons dried fennel seeds

1 egg

½ cup heavy whipping cream

Instructions

Preheat oven to 425°F. Prepare a baking sheet by covering it with parchment paper and coating with cooking spray.

Mix beer, warm water, and yeast; let sit until it bubbles, about 10 minutes. Add flour, salt, olive oil, and fennel seeds and mix in the bowl of an electric mixer fitted with a dough hook or knead by hand until smooth. Do not overmix or the dough will become tough. The dough should be slightly sticky, but still easy to form into a large ball. If it sticks to your fingers, add a little more flour. Place dough in a well-oiled mixing bowl and let rise in a warm place until it doubles in size, approximately 1 hour. While dough is rising, whisk the egg and heavy whipping cream together and set aside.

Once the dough has risen, gently punch it down and place onto a work surface coated lightly with cooking spray to prevent sticking. With a rolling pin, flatten dough evenly until it is ¼ inch thick. Cut across the width of the dough, making strips that are approximately 1 inch wide (a pizza cutter makes long, even strips). Using a light touch, roll each piece of dough by hand into rounded strips. Each strip will be quite long; cut as necessary to form 6- to 8-inch pieces. Place breadsticks on the baking sheet. Using a pastry brush, coat the breadsticks with the egg wash.

Bake for 15 to 20 minutes, rotating the baking sheet halfway through cooking, until breadsticks are a light golden brown. Serve with whipped butter.

Heirloom Bread ☀

This simple French bread is baked daily in the Chico kitchen and served at every table in the dining room. In the restaurant we prepare it in baguette form, long and thin, for uniformity. But at home you can be more creative—try braiding one loaf or twisting another to give this staple a decorative flair.

MAKES 2 LOAVES

Ingredients

8 cups bread flour
(a high-gluten flour)

1 tablespoon salt

3 cups warm water
(approximately 110°F)

2 teaspoons instant yeast

½ cup cornmeal

1 egg white

½ teaspoon salt

Instructions

Place flour, salt, water, and yeast into the bowl of an electric mixer fitted with a dough hook. If you are mixing the bread by hand, be sure to use swift, strong strokes to prevent overmixing. Combine ingredients thoroughly, adding more flour as necessary to achieve a soft, smooth texture. Knead for 10 minutes.

Move dough to a clean bowl (do not coat in oil) and cover with plastic wrap. Let rise until double in size, about 1 to 1½ hours. Gently punch down dough and divide into two equal pieces. Let rest for 5 minutes. Flatten each piece into an oval and form into desired shape. Be careful not to knead or handle it too much at this stage, because it will become tough. Place on a baking sheet sprinkled with cornmeal or into a French loaf bread pan. Cover and let rise until the loaves almost double in size, about 30 minutes.

Preheat oven to 425°F. Combine the egg white and salt; brush loaves generously with the mixture. Slash loaves diagonally with a sharp serrated knife in three or four places. Bake for 15 minutes, then reduce heat to 375°F. Bake 30 minutes more, until bread is golden and crusty.

Smoked Trout with Toasted Almond and Dill Cream Cheese and Tomato-Caper Relish ✹

The cooks at Chico rely on Paradise Valley's Trout Culture team to raise organic, local rainbow trout that is rich in flavor for this classic appetizer. Prepared daily, the fish is marinated in a curry, salt, and brown sugar brine with the skin intact, then slow-smoked over alder wood until it reaches firm, flaky perfection. The process takes two hours, but is well worth the effort to develop this flavor. For home preparation, it's simple to convert a barbecue grill into a smoker using soaked wood chips and a low temperature. Of course, you could also purchase smoked trout or substitute smoked salmon from a local grocer, but where's the fun in that?

SERVES 4–6

Ingredients

FOR THE TOASTED ALMOND AND DILL CREAM CHEESE:

Zest and juice of ½ lemon

2 tablespoons sliced toasted almonds

¼ cup sour cream

8 ounces cream cheese, room temperature

1 teaspoon minced fresh dill

½ teaspoon salt

FOR THE TOMATO-CAPER RELISH:

3 large Roma tomatoes, seeds removed, diced

1 small red onion, diced

¼ cup capers

¼ cup chopped fresh chives

2 tablespoons apple cider vinegar

2 tablespoons minced fresh parsley

Salt and freshly ground black pepper to taste

FOR THE TROUT AND BREAD:

4–5 ounces boneless Smoked Trout (recipe page 195).

1 loaf French bread or Chico Heirloom Bread (recipe page 43)

Instructions

TO PREPARE THE TOASTED ALMOND AND DILL CREAM CHEESE:
Thoroughly combine all ingredients together by hand or in a mixer until easy to spread. Chill until ready to serve.

TO PREPARE THE TOMATO-CAPER RELISH:
Mix all ingredients together. Chill until ready to serve.

TO SERVE:
Display the trout in one piece on a platter, with the cream cheese spread and the relish on the side with sliced fresh bread.

Smoked Trout Croquettes

Satisfyingly smoky, salty, and buttery, this is a simple appetizer that can easily be prepared in advance for serving at a dinner party.

MAKES ABOUT 14 PIECES

Ingredients

2 tablespoons finely diced shallot

3 tablespoons finely diced celery

¼ cup finely diced leeks

1 cup canola oil, divided

1½ pounds Yukon potatoes

1 tablespoon unsalted butter

⅓ cup heavy cream

2 teaspoons kosher salt

3 large eggs, divided

4 ounces Smoked Trout (recipe page 195)

1 cup all-purpose flour

1 cup panko bread crumbs

Instructions

Sweat shallots, celery, and leeks in a pan generously coated with canola oil. Meanwhile, peel and dice Yukons, then add to a large pot of water and boil until soft. Drain water from potatoes and use a fork or masher to mash the potatoes. Add butter, cream, shallots, celery, leeks, and salt, mashing and mixing until well combined. Place mixture in the refrigerator to cool for approximately 30 minutes to 1 hour.

Once the potatoes have cooled, mix in one egg and the smoked trout. Portion into 2-ounce cakes and cool in the freezer until stiff, at least 1 hour.

Set up a three-stage breading station: flour, egg wash, and panko. Bread the cakes with flour, then egg wash, and finally crust with panko. In a skillet, heat remaining canola oil (it should be about 1 inch deep) on medium-high. Test readiness by dropping a little panko in the pan; when it quickly fries to a golden color, the oil is the perfect temperature. Carefully place croquettes in the pan; avoid crowding the pieces in order to keep the oil temperature consistent. Fry on both sides until golden brown.

Serve on a bed of fresh garden greens with your dressing of choice, such as the Orange-Ginger Vinaigrette (recipe page 84). Other complimentary sauces include the Roasted Tomato Hollandaise (recipe page 29) or the Smoked Corn-Quinoa-Black Bean Salsa (recipe page 127).

Artichokes with Curry Aioli ☀

In the 1970s and 1980s artichokes were considered exotic and were not commonly found in grocery stores. During this period, a chilled artichoke was a complimentary starter during dinner in Chico's historic dining room. Served with a touch of curried mayo, it is a simple, but memorable, *amuse bouche*.

SERVES 4–8

Ingredients

FOR THE ARTICHOKES:
4 large artichokes

FOR THE CURRY AIOLI:
1 cup mayonnaise

1 tablespoon mild yellow curry

Instructions

TO PREPARE THE ARTICHOKES:
Cut stems if desired. (The stems taste as good as the heart, so you can also leave them.) Trim the thorny tips of the outside leaves with scissors, and with a serrated knife slice off the top. Place artichokes in a steaming basket over 1 to 2 inches of boiling water. Cook covered until tender, about 25 to 35 minutes for medium artichokes and up to 45 minutes for large artichokes. Test for tender readiness by plucking a leaf from the middle of the vegetable; if it pulls out easily, artichokes are done. Chill for at least 1 hour in the refrigerator.

TO PREPARE THE CURRY AIOLI:
Combine mayonnaise and curry, then whisk until thoroughly combined.

TO SERVE:
Cut chilled artichokes into quarters and scoop out the fuzzy portion at the center of the artichoke, but be sure not to cut any of the treasured heart, the best part. Lay sliced-side down on a plate. Spoon the Curry Aioli into a small side dish or ramekin for dipping and serve.

Baked Brie
with Huckleberry Coulis and Hollandaise Sauce

There are about forty species of huckleberries, all native to North America. In Montana the black huckleberry, dark purple in color, is the most widespread. Huckleberries are difficult to come by, even in Montana; appropriate substitutes in this dish are lingonberry, currant, or blackberry preserves. Regardless of which fruit you choose, what is essential for this starter is that the berry sauce balances the creamy hollandaise with a precise sweetness and tartness. Timing is also key; the baked Brie and sauces should be served immediately.

SERVES 4–6

Ingredients

FOR THE HUCKLEBERRY COULIS:

1 cup huckleberry preserves

Zest of 1 orange

½ cup cranberry juice

FOR THE BAKED BRIE:

8 ounces Brie cheese

4 (5 x 5-inch) premade puff pastry sheets (available at most grocery stores in the frozen dessert section)

3 eggs

¼ cup half-and-half

FOR SERVING:

1 loaf of French bread or Chico Heirloom Bread (recipe page 43)

1 cup Hollandaise Sauce (recipe page 188)

Instructions

TO PREPARE THE HUCKLEBERRY COULIS:

Place all ingredients into a blender or food processor and puree until smooth. Set aside.

TO PREPARE THE BAKED BRIE:

Preheat oven to 450°F. Line a baking sheet with parchment paper.

Trim the rind of the Brie so that only the soft, creamy portion remains. For a shared appetizer use the whole piece, but for individual mini-Bries, cut cheese into four 2-ounce squares. Gently wrap the pastry around the cheese as if you were wrapping a present; with your fingers crease the folds of the pastry to smooth and secure the dough.

Beat the eggs and half-and-half until mixed thoroughly for an egg wash. (This will prevent the puff pastry from burning in the oven.) Dip each pastry-wrapped Brie in the egg wash and place on the baking sheet. Bake until golden brown, about 15 to 20 minutes. The cheese should be melted in the center of the pastry. Check for doneness by inserting a toothpick into the center of the pastry; if the toothpick comes out clean, the Brie is done.

Cut bread diagonally into 1-inch slices, cover, and reserve until ready to serve.

TO SERVE:

Pour the hollandaise sauce onto an oversize platter or four individual serving plates, covering the surfaces completely. Next, drizzle huckleberry coulis in parallel lines to create decorative stripes over the hollandaise sauce. Place baked Brie squares on top of sauce. Serve the sliced bread on another plate or around the edge of the serving dish.

Wild Mushroom Bruschetta
with Smoked Chèvre

Wild mushrooms are a seasonal delicacy that brings the local foragers to the back door of the restaurant kitchen when they have a big crop. Springtime morels can draw $30 per pound, and autumn chanterelles are coveted for their nutty flavor. This recipe marries earthy wild mushroom tones with the wood-smoked tanginess of warm, creamy chèvre, a combination that is reminiscent of the habitat where these wild fungi are often found. The recipe calls for eight ounces of cheese, but don't be afraid to use as much chèvre as you would like.

SERVES 8

Ingredients

¼ cup diced shallot

1 tablespoon olive oil

4 cloves garlic, diced

3 cups sliced wild mushrooms

1 cup white wine

1 tablespoon unsalted butter

2 tablespoons chopped fresh parsley, divided

Salt and freshly ground black pepper to taste

Crostini (recipe page 187)

8 ounces Smoked Chèvre (recipe page 195)

Instructions

In a large skillet, sweat shallots and garlic in a little olive oil over medium heat. Add mushrooms and continue to cook until softened. Once the shallots begin to caramelize, deglaze the pan with wine, stirring the mixture. Simmer until wine has reduced by half. Turn off heat, then add butter and 1 tablespoon parsley. Stir until butter has melted into the wine and thickened the sauce. Salt and pepper to taste.

Spoon mushroom mixture onto crostinis. Crumble smoked chèvre on top and garnish with remaining parsley.

Pan-Seared Scallops
with Curry Sauce over Moroccan Salsa

This can be served as a light appetizer for a small group or split as an entree for two. The creamy curry and the sweet crunch of the salsa is a flavorful marriage with large buttery scallops seared to perfection.

SERVES 4-6

Ingredients

FOR THE MOROCCAN SALSA:

1 cup dried apricots, julienned

½ red onion, small diced

4 green onions, sliced thin

1 red pepper, small diced

1 cup black olives, sliced thin

FOR THE CURRY SAUCE:

1 tablespoon sesame oil

3 shallots, minced

2 tablespoons green curry paste

1 cup white wine

¼ cup lime juice

4 cups unsweetened coconut milk

1 cup cream of coconut (such as Coco Lopez brand)

FOR THE SCALLOPS:

12 large sea scallops (u/10)

1 tablespoon unsalted butter

Instructions

TO MAKE THE MOROCCAN SALSA:

Combine all ingredients in a bowl and mix thoroughly. Chill until ready to serve.

TO MAKE THE CURRY SAUCE:

In a saucepan combine the oil, shallots, and curry paste and cook over medium heat until the curry paste starts to brown. Deglaze with the wine and lime juice, then cook until reduced by half. Add coconut milk and cream of coconut and reduce by half again. Store in a covered container until ready for use.

TO COOK THE SCALLOPS:

Rinse scallops and pat dry with a paper towel. In a cast-iron or stainless steel skillet, melt butter over medium-high heat and evenly coat the pan. Set scallops into the super-hot pan (test with a few flecks of water that should sizzle upon contact) about 1 inch apart; you may need to cook in two batches. Cook for 2 minutes until scallops are golden brown and easily release with a spatula. Flip each scallop and cook for another 2 minutes. Remove scallops from the pan and set on a warm plate.

TO SERVE:

Ladle curry sauce onto a large platter, then spoon twelve separate mounds of Moroccan salsa on top of the sauce. Place one scallop on each mound for an elegant share appetizer.

BBQ Bison Short Rib Ravioli
with Sweet Corn Cream Sauce

This classic Chico recipe was developed by former chef Morgan Milton to create a balance between the earthy sweetness of corn and barbecue sauce and the hearty bison flavors. Relying on Montana-sourced bison and local microbrew Moose Drool from Bozeman Brewing Co., along with fresh corn and a toothsome house-made pasta, this multistep dish is worth the effort. To cut down on kitchen time, prepare the short ribs and barbecue sauce one day in advance.

SERVES 6 (MAKES ABOUT 25 RAVIOLIS)

Ingredients

FOR THE RAVIOLI DOUGH:

2 cups all-purpose flour

¼ teaspoon kosher salt

2 large eggs plus 2 egg yolks, beaten

FOR THE RAVIOLI FILLING:

2 pounds bison short ribs

2 tablespoons vegetable oil

2 cans Coca-Cola

Moose Drool BBQ Sauce (recipe page 189)

FOR THE SWEET CORN CREAM SAUCE:

2 cups sweet corn kernels

½ yellow onion, small diced

1 tablespoon vegetable oil

1 tablespoon apple cider vinegar

Salt and freshly ground black pepper to taste

1½ cups heavy cream

FOR THE CHILI OIL, FRIED CARROTS, AND GREEN ONIONS GARNISH:

1½ cups vegetable oil, divided (1 cup for chili oil, ½ cup for fried carrots)

1 tablespoon red pepper flakes

½ tablespoon cayenne pepper

1 large carrot

2 green onions

Instructions

TO MAKE THE RAVIOLI DOUGH:

Place flour and salt into a large bowl, forming a well in the center. Pour the beaten eggs into the well of flour and mix with a wooden spoon until combined into a shaggy dough. Turn dough onto a lightly floured surface and knead for approximately 10 minutes until it forms a smooth ball. Divide dough into four pieces. Flatten each into a 1-inch-thick disk and wrap individually in plastic wrap; let rest for 1 to 3 hours at room temperature.

Using a rolling pin (on a lightly floured surface) or a pasta machine, roll each piece of dough until it is as thin as possible, not quite paper thin (for a pasta machine, it would be at a setting of 3 or less). When each sheet is complete, stack with a light dusting of flour as you begin to assemble the raviolis.

TO PREPARE THE RAVIOLI FILLING:

Preheat oven to 325°F. Heat a large cast-iron skillet over high heat, letting the pan get very hot. Season the meat with salt and pepper. Add enough vegetable oil to coat the bottom of the pan, then sear the ribs on all four sides. Place seared ribs into a dutch oven or braising pan. Pour Coca-Cola over ribs, return to the stove, and bring to a boil. Cover braising pan and place in oven. Braise ribs for 2½ hours, or until tender.

Remove ribs from pan and strain the liquid through a fine-mesh strainer into a medium-size pot. Heat bison pan juices on the stove over medium-high heat until reduced by half; set aside. When the meat has cooled enough to work with, remove the bones along with any fat or sinew. Pull the meat into "shreds" with a fork or your fingers; there should be no large pieces, just even shreds. Add reduced liquid to shredded meat, than add a generous amount of Moose Drool BBQ sauce so the meat is well coated, mixing with a fork. Let cool and set aside. This mixture can be made up to 3 days in advance of service.

TO ASSEMBLE THE RAVIOLI:

Lay one sheet of pasta onto a flat work surface; keep the unused piece covered to prevent it from drying out. Using a tablespoon, mound the ravioli filling in a row down the pasta sheet, leaving 1 inch of space between each spoonful. Scoop approximately twenty-four spoonfuls onto dough. Lay the second sheet of dough over the top of the filling. With your fingers, seal the filling into the dough. Run a pizza cutter down the length of the dough and then across each row to cut squares, being careful not to cut too close to the filling to prevent raviolis from bursting when they are cooked. Crimp the edges of each square to seal. Repeat this process with the remaining two pieces of pasta. Cook immediately, refrigerate in a covered container for same- or next-day use, or freeze for up to 1 month.

TO COOK THE RAVIOLI:

Bring a large pot of water to a boil and add 1 teaspoon vegetable oil per quart of water and salt if desired. Add raviolis to boiling water; do not stir. Return water to a boil and cook 5 to 7 minutes, until texture of the pasta is to your liking; remove with a slotted spoon or pour into a strainer in the sink.

TO MAKE THE SWEET CORN CREAM SAUCE:

In a skillet on high heat, add corn, onions, oil, vinegar, salt, and pepper and cook until onions and corn are soft. Add cream and continue to cook until thickened.

TO MAKE THE CHILI OIL:

Combine the 1 cup oil, red pepper flakes, and cayenne pepper in a small pot and bring to a simmer over medium heat. Remove from heat and allow to cool, then strain through a fine-mesh strainer. Chili oil will keep for up to a year and is a handy addition to other sauces, grilled vegetables, and meats or other types of pasta. A little goes a long way, so drizzle with care to add a warm, spicy flavor.

TO MAKE THE FRIED CARROTS:

Peel skin off the carrot. Using a vegetable peeler, slice the carrot into very thin slices from top to bottom. In a medium-size skillet, heat the ½ cup oil on medium high. Fry carrots in hot oil until brown and crispy. Remove from oil and place on a paper towel to absorb excess oil. Reserve until service.

TO SERVE:

Ladle sweet corn cream sauce into a serving bowl or platter. Place raviolis on top of the cream sauce, drizzle with chili oil, then top with fried carrots and small slices of green onion cut on the bias.

CHEF'S TIP

Poaching

The old-fashioned method of slow-cooking in liquid works best with a generous dose of patience. To ensure the desired tenderness, starting with cold water is essential. Allowing the poaching liquid to gradually reach barely a boil takes more time than most of us are accustomed to, but the extra minutes are the key to success here.

FOR THE POACHING LIQUID:

4–5 cups cold water
2 bay leaves
1 clove garlic
¼ teaspoon whole red peppercorns
Submerge ballotine in cold water in a medium-size pot. Season with bay leaves, garlic, and peppercorns. Over medium heat, bring the poaching liquid to a bare simmer (add patience here). Once it reaches that bare boil, turn to low heat and allow to poach for 20 minutes. Remove from liquid and prepare according to main recipe.

Cornish Game Hen Ballotine
with Balsamic Fig Reduction

This is a bit of a challenging preparation, but worth the effort. Essentially, it is a new variation of an old gourmet preparation of forcemeat rolled inside the boneless form of a game hen with the skin intact. It entails using the remaining meat and fat scraps trimmed from the whole duck you presumably made recently (Duck Grand Marnier Two Ways, recipe page 121) and requires a meat grinder. If you are not yet daunted, then this is the culinary challenge for you.

SERVES 4

Ingredients

FOR THE CORNISH HENS:

2 Cornish game hens

8 ounces duck scrap, chilled (trimmed fat and meat from Duck Grand Marnier Two Ways, recipe page 121)

⅓ cup cremini mushrooms

1 tablespoon chopped shallot

⅛ teaspoon nutmeg

⅛ teaspoon juniper berries

½ teaspoon allspice

½ teaspoon kosher salt

FOR THE BALSAMIC FIG REDUCTION SAUCE:

½ cup diced dried figs

¼ cup granulated sugar

2 cups red wine

2 tablespoons balsamic vinegar

Instructions

TO PREPARE THE CORNISH HENS:

Starting on the hens' backs, cut the flesh and skin away from the bones, being careful to keep the skin intact, discarding the wings and legs (reserve bones and legs for stock; see Chicken Stock recipe page 184). Wrap in plastic and refrigerate until ready to roll with the forcemeat.

Combine the duck trim with mushrooms, shallots, and spices in a food processor until thoroughly mixed, but still chunky rather than smooth. Chill forcemeat in the refrigerator for about an hour. Keeping the poultry and forcemeat chilled will make it easy to form into rolls. While the forcemeat chills, make the balsamic fig reduction sauce.

TO MAKE THE BALSAMIC FIG REDUCTION SAUCE:

Combine all ingredients in a saucepan. Bring to a boil, then reduce to a simmer. Simmer until sauce coats the back of a spoon. Reserve for dinner service. Sauce can be made a day ahead and keeps for up to 2 weeks in a sealed container at room temperature.

TO MAKE THE BALLOTINE:

Remove chilled hens and forcemeat from the refrigerator. Lay hens onto a flat surface, skin-side down. Divide the forcemeat equally between the hens and roll up into logs. Tie with butcher twine. Sous vide at 140°F for 1½ hours (See "Cooking Techniques" for details, page 196); alternatively, you can opt to poach the ballotine (see Chef's Tip on previous page).

TO ASSEMBLE:

Heat a skillet with a small amount of oil. Place ballotines in the pan and sear all sides. To serve, slice the ballotine and arrange as a fan; finish with the balsamic fig reduction. This is great served over the Red Lentil Puree (recipe page 90).

Ahi Wonton
with Avocado Slaw and Citrus Chili Aioli

Celebrating the abundant access to the freshest ingredients, Chef Dave Wells brings an Asian flair to this appetizer. While the spiral of fried wonton makes actually eating the deconstructed wonton seem daunting, there is added pleasure in shattering its perfection to mix in the crunch with the velvety fresh ahi and avocado slaw with the first bite.

SERVES 8

Ingredients

FOR THE TUNA WONTONS:
1 package wonton wrappers

8 ounces sushi grade ahi

FOR THE CITRUS CHILI AIOLI:
2 egg yolks

2 cloves garlic

Juice of ½ lemon and ½ lime

1 cup canola oil

2 fresh jalapeños

1 tablespoon chopped cilantro

Zest of 1 lemon and 1 lime

Salt to taste

FOR THE AVOCADO SLAW:
2 scallions

¼ cup cilantro

1 red bell pepper

1 avocado, finely diced

⅛ teaspoon cumin

Juice of ½ lime

Salt to taste

Instructions

TO PREPARE THE WONTONS:
Cut wontons into strips. Moisten with water and wrap around a ring mold. Tie with butcher's twine. Fry in a deep fryer at 350°F until golden brown. Take off twine and gently remove the wonton from the ring mold to reveal a delicate spiral. (For a simpler option, simply fry wonton strips in 2 inches of canola oil over medium-high heat in a large pan.)

TO PREPARE THE AIOLI:
In a food processor, combine egg yolks, garlic, and citrus juice. Run processor on high until the yolks are whipped and fluffy. Slowly drizzle in oil until emulsified. Seed the jalapeños and dice fine. Fold jalapeños into aioli with the cilantro and citrus zest. Salt to taste.

TO PREPARE THE AHI:
Heat a skillet with a couple of tablespoons of canola oil. Salt the ahi. When pan starts to smoke, add ahi and sear both sides, cooking the fish rare. Slice the fish into thin slices.

TO PREPARE THE SLAW:
Finely julienne the scallions, cilantro, and bell pepper. Combine with avocado, cumin, lime juice, and salt to taste.

TO ASSEMBLE:
Spoon a teaspoon of aioli on the plate and place a wonton vertically on the aioli. Spoon a little slaw into the round of the wonton and place a slice of ahi on top.

Quail Eggs
with Roasted Asparagus and Nduja

This is an uncommon combination of flavors. The salty, crunchy, and smooth texture of these three simple components creates a satisfying teaser at the start of a fine meal.

SERVES 6

Ingredients

1 tablespoon canola oil

6 quail eggs

6 asparagus tips

6 ounces nduja (a spicy, spreadable salumi; a chorizo spread [see below] can be substituted)

1 tablespoon olive oil

Salt to taste

Instructions

In a hot skillet that is lightly oiled with canola oil, fry the quail eggs sunny-side up. Slice the asparagus tips in half and toss with a little olive oil and salt. Roast at 400°F until tender, about 5 to 10 minutes.

Spread 1 ounce of nduja on the plate, stack two halves of asparagus, and top with a quail egg.

CHEF'S TIP

Note: If you can't find nduja, you can replace it with the following:

7 ounces Spanish chorizo

2–3 tablespoons olive oil

Dice the chorizo and place in food processor. Process and add oil until the chorizo becomes a smooth paste.

Mussels with Caramelized Onion, Bacon, Apple, and Lemon-Thyme Cream Sauce

The preparation of freshly steamed mussels varies in the dining room each evening based on seasonal ingredients. A bright cream sauce never disappoints, and in this recipe the balance of cream with a hint of tanginess from the lemon and apple accompanies the rustic flavors of onion and bacon beautifully.

SERVES 6–8

Ingredients

½ cup diced bacon

1½ cups julienned yellow onion

2 Granny Smith apples, diced

2 pounds mussels

1 cup white wine

1 cup half-and-half

2 tablespoons lemon juice

1 tablespoon fresh thyme

Salt to taste

Instructions

Render the diced bacon in a large skillet over medium-high heat. Remove when crispy. Caramelize onions in the bacon fat. Add apples and sauté for a few minutes until slightly softened, then add bacon and mussels. Deglaze with wine, being sure to scrape up all the fond from the pan with a wooden spoon. Reduce by half. Add half-and-half and simmer for a few more minutes, then add lemon juice and thyme. Salt to taste.

Serve with crusty bread or Fennel Breadsticks (recipe page 41).

Oysters Rockefeller ☀

Chico started serving this timeless hors d'oeuvre in 1976. It was a delicacy in Montana at the time, since fresh seafood was not readily available. Fresh oysters were flown in once a week to Billings (about 200 miles away), and the owners would go pick up the order. Today, with fresh seafood flown into Bozeman regularly and delivered to Chico, it's much easier to offer oysters on the menu.

SERVES 6

Ingredients

2 slices bacon, julienned

1 large yellow onion, diced

2 tablespoons minced garlic

2 cups fresh spinach, julienned

1 tablespoon anisette liqueur

¾ cup heavy whipping cream

2 dozen raw oysters on the half shell

¼ cup grated Parmesan cheese

2 cups coarse rock salt

¾ cup Hollandaise Sauce (recipe page 188)

Instructions

Preheat oven to 450°F. Render julienned bacon in a large sauté pan. Add onions and cook until translucent. Combine garlic, spinach, anisette, and cream; mix with bacon and onions. Cook until spinach is wilted. Remove from heat.

Place oysters on a baking sheet and spoon 1 heaping teaspoon of the spinach mixture onto each oyster, then sprinkle with Parmesan. Bake until spinach mixture browns on top, about 8 minutes. While the oysters are cooking, quickly prepare a platter with a bed of coarse salt. Remove oysters from the oven and gently place them onto the salt. Top each oyster with a dollop of hollandaise sauce, about ½ teaspoon and serve warm.

SUMMER GARDEN GATHERING

WHEN THE GARDEN IS AT ITS ZENITH, everything feels right in the world. Among the tidy rows of kale, carrots, and kohlrabi, at 5,200 feet above sea level, the impossible seems possible. A path wanders through roses, irises, blooming plum trees, and friendly daisies to a bench that beckons peace. The raspberry bushes fruit happily, most often to the delight of guests strolling along the fence line. Could there be anything better than a fresh berry plucked and popped directly into your mouth?

Inside the greenhouses is a tropical elixir of humidity and warmth from April to November. The perfume of basil wafts across the forest of trellised tomato vines, and a banana tree flourishes. The soil is warmed and irrigated by the geothermal runoff from the natural hot springs pool. Butterflies and ladybugs flit in through the vents while the fan hums the perfect ambient sound. A team of dedicated Chico gardeners tend the crops and the flowers. It's hard, dirty work, but each of them beam Cheshire cat smiles as they labor. They know the garden's secrets.

Those gardener smiles invite us and offer the lush green as the perfect place for a garden gathering. The cool of the shade, a quaint cluster of tables on the grass, and the glide of the swing are a sweet promise. The setting is best paired with music, Montana Mules, and lemonade, all in the company of good friends.

Soups, Salads, and Sides

EITHER AS A SOLO MEAL OR AS THE bookends to the main course, soups, salads, and side dishes deserve their own show. Some chefs consider soup the true measure of a cook—a one-pot concoction of flavor, texture, and technique. A salad, especially fresh-picked from the Chico garden, can define a meal. As the small preparations that accompany a main course, veggies and starches often take a secondary position but, given care in pairing and preparation, can elevate a good meal.

Note: Recipes denoted by are Chico "Classics."

White Bean and Kale Soup
with Pistou

This Provençal-inspired soup is a wonderful vehicle for the abundant varieties of kale from the hot springs garden. It is a quick, savory meal that gains most of its flavor from the essential pistou that is added generously just before a bowl is placed before you. Often called the French version of pesto, but without the nuts, this versatile sauce adds an elegant layer of flavor to any soup. It is a subtle sauce that can also be paired easily with grilled meats and vegetables.

SERVES 8

Ingredients

FOR THE SOUP:

2 tablespoons olive oil

1 pound Italian sausage

1 large onion, diced

1 cup white wine

8 cups chicken stock

2 bay leaves

3 cups cooked cannellini beans

1 bunch kale, stemmed and chopped

Salt and freshly ground black pepper to taste

FOR THE PISTOU:

2 cups fresh basil

⅔ cup grated Parmesan cheese

4 cloves garlic

½ cup extra-virgin olive oil

Salt to taste

Instructions

TO MAKE THE SOUP:

In a large saucepan warm olive oil over medium-low heat, add Italian sausage. Once sausage is cooked, add onions and cook until slightly caramelized. Deglaze with the wine, careful to scrape up all the fond with a wooden spoon. Let wine reduce by half, then add stock and bay leaves. Simmer for 30 minutes, then add beans. Simmer for 10 more minutes, then add kale. When kale is cooked, but still slightly crunchy, season with salt and pepper.

TO PREPARE THE PISTOU:

Process basil, cheese, and garlic in a food processor to make a paste. Using a rubber spatula, scrape the mixture into a separate medium-size bowl. Whisk the olive oil into the mixture and season with salt to taste. Pistou can be made 2 days in advance; cover and refrigerate until ready to use.

TO SERVE:

Ladle soup into bowls and top with a dollop of pistou.

Chilled Beet, Ginger, and Coconut Milk Soup

Inspired by Chico's large kitchen garden and apiary, Chef Dave Wells developed this brightly flavored soup to showcase the beauty of Montana beets and the busy bees that yield golden honey each season. Best served chilled, it embodies the freshness of the summer season.

SERVES 6

Ingredients

3 medium-size beets

1 each orange, lime, and lemon

1 to 2 cups vegetable stock

4 cups coconut milk, divided (1 cup reserved for reduction)

2 tablespoons honey

2 tablespoons grated ginger

Salt to taste

Instructions

Peel and dice beets, then place in a medium saucepan. Zest each citrus fruit and add to beets. Then juice each citrus fruit directly into the saucepan. Add enough stock to cover beets and bring to a simmer. As beets simmer, check stock and add more occasionally to be sure beets remain covered with liquid. Simmer 40 to 45 minutes, until beets are tender.

Meanwhile, in a separate saucepan add 1 cup coconut milk and heat on medium-high. Reduce by half until it thickens into a sauce. Chill until ready to serve soup.

Once beets are cooked, transfer with their liquid to a blender. Add a cup of coconut milk, honey, and ginger. Blend until the mixture becomes a smooth puree. Add remaining 2 cups coconut milk, blend lightly, and salt to taste.

Chill the soup in the refrigerator for at least an hour. Serve cold with a small spoonful of the reduced coconut milk.

French Onion Soup ☀
with Gruyère Crouton

It is hard to beat this timeless classic of sweet onions sautéed and simmered with red wine, then topped with the rich sharpness of Gruyére cheese. It is a wonderful autumn preparation and a lovely beginning to a hearty meal. Prepare the beef stock a day in advance.

SERVES 8

Ingredients

2 tablespoons canola oil

8 cups julienned Walla Walla onions (substitute yellow if unavailable)

2 cups Burgundy or other red wine

¼ cup balsamic vinegar

4 quarts Beef Stock (recipe page 184)

Bouquet garni (a bundle of fresh herbs that includes a bay leaf, 3 sprigs of thyme, and about 6 sprigs of parsley all neatly tied with kitchen string)

Salt to taste

1 baguette

½ cup (1 stick) unsalted butter

1 cup grated Gruyère cheese

Instructions

Lightly oil a saucepan. Slowly cook onions over low heat (about an hour) until they are softened and brown. Turn heat up to medium-high to caramelize onions, then deglaze with wine and balsamic. Simmer over low heat and reduce the liquid by two-thirds. Add beef stock and bouquet garni. Simmer and reduce by a third. Salt to taste.

For the Gruyère crouton, slice the baguette on a bias into 2-inch-thick slices. Melt butter in a pan over medium heat. Add baguette and toast both sides in butter. Transfer to a baking sheet and cover slices in Gruyère. Gratinée under the broiler.

To serve, spoon soup into bowls and add crouton. Alternatively, pour soup into oven-safe crocks, add crouton, cover with Gruyère, and gratinée under the broiler.

Seafood Bisque ☾

This rich, creamy soup is an easy backdrop for the wonderful flavors of lobster and shrimp. The tomato paste provides a lovely color and a tangy flavor to balance the cream.

SERVES 4

Ingredients

2 small lobster tails
(5 ounces each)

1 dozen large shrimp

2 shallots, diced

4 tablespoons (½ stick)
unsalted butter

¼ cup white wine or sherry

4 cups Seafood Stock
(recipe page 185)

¼ cup tomato paste

1 pint heavy whipping cream

1 tablespoon chopped fresh
dill

2 tablespoons chopped
parsley, divided
(1 tablespoon reserved
for garnish)

2 tablespoons paprika

Juice of 1 lemon

Salt and white pepper to
taste

4 Crostini (recipe page 187)

Instructions

Clean and shell lobster and shrimp; reserve shells for stock. Refrigerate seafood until just before serving.

Prepare the seafood stock with the addition of lobster shells for more flavor.

In a large stockpot, sauté shallots in butter until softened, then add wine or sherry and seafood stock. Whisk tomato paste into stock until combined. Bring to a boil over medium-high heat. Add cream, dill, parsley, and paprika, whisking lightly. Simmer for 20 minutes over medium heat, making sure it does not boil or the cream will scald. Add lemon juice and salt and white pepper to taste. Simmer on low until ready to serve.

Steam shelled lobster tails over boiling water until edges appear red and meat is white (4 to 5 minutes). Steam shrimp in the same pot until they turn pink. Slice lobsters into ½-inch-thick medallions and divide among shallow serving bowls; ladle soup over lobster. Place a crostini and three shrimp per bowl on top of soup and garnish with a sprinkling of chopped parsley.

Wild Mushroom Bisque ☀

Spring brings wild morels and oyster mushrooms bursting from the forest floors throughout the region. If you are lucky, you might catch a string of special dishes on the dining room menu prepared with an assortment of fresh fungi. This is the best of those savory recipes.

SERVES 6

Ingredients

¼ pound fresh oyster mushrooms, stemmed and chopped

¼ pound fresh portobello mushrooms, grilled and chopped

2 large leeks, cleaned and chopped

½ large yellow onion, chopped

2 tablespoons minced garlic

½ cup sherry

2 quarts Chicken Stock (recipe page 184; make this the day before)

2 cups heavy whipping cream

¼ pound fresh morels, stemmed (substitute dried if necessary)

2 tablespoons unsalted butter

1 teaspoon fresh thyme leaves, plus extra sprigs for garnish

Salt and freshly ground black pepper to taste

Crostini (recipe page 187)

¼ cup shaved Parmesan cheese

Instructions

In a large stockpot, sauté fresh oyster and grilled portobello mushrooms, leeks, onion, and garlic until soft and browning. Deglaze with sherry. Add chicken stock and stir in cream. Simmer over medium heat until reduced by one-third (about 45 minutes). Puree and return to the pot; simmer on low heat.

In a separate saucepan, sauté whole morels in butter, add 1 teaspoon thyme leaves, and salt and pepper to taste. Serve soup with crostini and top with sautéed morels, shaved Parmesan, and extra sprigs of thyme for garnish.

CHEF'S TIP

If substituting dried morels, rehydrate approximately 1 cup of mushrooms.

Roasted Red Pepper Soup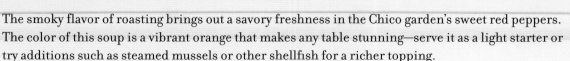

The smoky flavor of roasting brings out a savory freshness in the Chico garden's sweet red peppers. The color of this soup is a vibrant orange that makes any table stunning—serve it as a light starter or try additions such as steamed mussels or other shellfish for a richer topping.

SERVES 8

Ingredients

8 large red bell peppers

4 cups ice water (for ice bath)

2 quarts Chicken Stock (recipe page 184; make the day before)

Canola oil (to coat the pan)

2 large yellow onions, peeled and sliced

1 large carrot, peeled and rough chopped

4 large shallots, rough chopped

1 large tomato, rough diced

2 stalks celery, rough diced

2 cloves garlic, rough diced

½ cup white wine

1 cup heavy whipping cream

¼ teaspoon saffron

Juice of 1 lemon

Salt and freshly ground black pepper to taste

¼ cup minced fresh chives, for garnish

Instructions

If making your own roasted red peppers, roast whole red bell peppers over an open flame on a gas stovetop or barbecue grill, blackening the skin. When mostly blackened, using tongs, remove each pepper from flame and immerse in an ice bath to remove the outer layer of skin. When skin is removed, seed peppers and rough chop. Alternatively, peppers can be roasted in a 400°F oven on a cookie sheet for 10 to 15 minutes. Set aside.

In a large stockpot, bring chicken stock to a boil. Add roasted red peppers and simmer.

Coat a saucepan with canola oil and warm over medium heat, then add onions, carrot, shallots, tomato, celery, and garlic. Sauté until the ingredients are softened, then add ½ cup white wine to deglaze. Stir and add mixture to the chicken stock. Simmer over medium-high heat for 1½ hours, stirring occasionally.

Puree mixture in a blender (may need to do it in two or three batches) until smooth. Return to stockpot over low heat. Whisk in heavy whipping cream, saffron, and lemon juice. Add salt and pepper to taste; simmer another 10 minutes. Serve in generous bowls and garnish with chives.

Classic Spinach Salad

This recipe appeared in a 1988 issue of *Bon Appétit* and is Chico's signature salad. Grown in the garden behind the restaurant, fresh spinach is coated with a creamy dressing to give it a rich flavor.

SERVES 4

Ingredients

FOR THE CREAMY ITALIAN DRESSING:

1 cup mayonnaise

2 tablespoons Italian herb seasoning

2 tablespoons granulated garlic

1 teaspoon granulated sugar

1 tablespoon extra-virgin olive oil

2 tablespoons red wine vinegar

1½ cups half-and-half

FOR THE SALAD:

1 pound spinach

1 small red onion, thinly sliced

½ cup chopped cooked bacon

2 eggs, hard boiled and chopped

Instructions

TO PREPARE THE CREAMY ITALIAN DRESSING:

Blend mayonnaise, Italian seasoning, garlic, and sugar in a blender. With machine running, slowly drizzle in olive oil and then vinegar. Gradually add half-and-half and blend until smooth. Chill until needed.

TO ASSEMBLE:

In a large bowl, toss dressing with spinach and onion until leaves are coated. Divide among plates and top with bacon and eggs.

Garden Crudo with Fresh Citronette

Light and beautifully simple, this is a salad that celebrates the garden, the summer season, and the essence of fresh ingredients. Chef Dave Wells lets each ingredient shine in its purest raw form.

SERVES 4

Ingredients

1 small yellow squash

1 small zucchini

1 cup grape or cherry tomatoes

Juice and zest of 1 lemon

¼ cup extra-virgin olive oil

Salt to taste

1 teaspoon fresh thyme

1 teaspoon fresh parsley

1 tablespoon edible flowers (such as coriander, pansies, nasturtiums, or marigolds)

Instructions

Using a vegetable peeler, shave squash and zucchini into thin "planks." Halve the tomatoes. Combine lemon juice, zest, and olive oil to make a citronette. Toss the vegetables gently with the citronette and season with salt. Roll each squash plank into individual cylinders. Place each cylinder vertically on a platter and spoon the tomatoes next to the squash. Garnish with fresh thyme, parsley, and flowers. Drizzle any remaining dressing over vegetables and serve with a crisp white wine.

Caesar Salad ☀

This is a special Caesar dressing—uncommonly thick and creamy, the anchovy and garlic flavors are evenly balanced as they coat. Serve it as a dinner salad or top with grilled chicken, salmon, or steak for a meal.

SERVES 8 (MAKES 2 CUPS DRESSING)

Ingredients

1 egg yolk

Juice of 1 lemon

½ ounce (4) anchovies

2 tablespoons Dijon mustard

3 cloves garlic

1½ cups extra-virgin olive oil

½ cup grated Parmesan cheese

2 teaspoons black pepper

1 pound Romaine lettuce, washed

¼ cup shaved Parmesan cheese

1 cup croutons

Instructions

Combine egg yolk, lemon juice, anchovies, mustard, and garlic and puree in a food processor or blender. With machine running, slowly drizzle in olive oil until mixture is the consistency of mayonnaise; drizzling the oil is important to keep the full, creamy texture. Transfer to a bowl and add Parmesan and pepper. Mix thoroughly. Dressing keeps for 2 days in the refrigerator.

Tear lettuce into bite-size pieces and place in a large bowl. Before serving, toss lettuce with dressing until generously coated. Divide onto plates and top with shaved Parmesan and croutons.

Mixed Greens ☀
with Orange-Ginger Vinaigrette

Simple, sweet, and refreshing, this light salad dressing is one of the most requested recipes by guests at Chico. Through the years it has become a nostalgic favorite. For best flavor, prepare the vinaigrette a day or two in advance of serving this salad.

SERVES 8 (MAKES 1 CUP DRESSING)

Ingredients

FOR THE ORANGE-GINGER
VINAIGRETTE:

Zest of 1 orange

Juice of 1 orange

1 tablespoon lemon juice

1 teaspoon minced fresh ginger

⅓ cup red wine vinegar

Freshly ground black pepper

2 tablespoons granulated sugar

⅓ cup canola oil

⅓ cup extra-virgin olive oil

FOR THE SALAD:

1 pound mixed greens

1 carrot, peeled and grated

2 cherry tomatoes

¼ cup sliced scallions

1 cup croutons

Instructions

TO PREPARE THE ORANGE-GINGER VINAIGRETTE:
Combine orange zest and juice, lemon juice, ginger, red wine vinegar, black pepper, and sugar in a blender on high speed. Combine canola and olive oils; while machine is running, drizzle in oil mixture slowly and blend until emulsified. Let dressing sit at room temperature for 20 minutes, whisk it again before serving. This dressing can be made a week ahead; keep in the refrigerator. If the dressing has been refrigerated, allow it to come to room temperature again and shake well before serving.

TO ASSEMBLE:
Arrange greens on individual serving plates. Top with carrots, tomatoes, scallions, croutons, and orange-ginger vinaigrette.

Baby Kale with Warm Goat Cheese Medallions and Flathead Cherry-Mint Vinaigrette

Bitter greens are the landscape for a sweet, refreshing dressing complemented with the crunch of pistachios and the tang of warm, creamy goat cheese from local Amaltheia Dairy. Chef Brian Sukut uses kale and fresh mint from the geothermally heated greenhouse in this simple salad bursting with flavorful contrasts. This recipe is ideal to make ahead if you are entertaining. The dressing holds for two weeks, and the medallions can be prepared and chilled the day before.

SERVES 4

Ingredients

6 cups baby kale

FOR THE CHERRY-MINT VINAIGRETTE:

¼ cup fresh pitted Montana Flathead (Lambert variety) cherries

2 tablespoons balsamic vinegar

1 tablespoon sherry vinegar

2 tablespoons chopped fresh mint, plus extra for garnish

¼ cup extra-virgin olive oil

¼ cup sunflower oil

Salt and freshly ground black pepper to taste

FOR THE GOAT CHEESE MEDALLIONS:

4 ounces organic goat cheese from Amaltheia Dairy in Bozeman, Montana, or your local farm

¼ cup all-purpose flour

2 eggs, beaten

½ cup finely chopped pistachios

1 cup canola oil

Instructions

TO MAKE THE CHERRY-MINT VINAIGRETTE:
Combine cherries, vinegars, and mint in a blender and puree. When the ingredients are well blended, slowly add the olive oil and sunflower oil to emulsify the dressing to a light, creamy texture. Add salt and pepper to taste. Chill for an hour or more.

TO MAKE THE GOAT CHEESE MEDALLIONS:
Begin with chilled goat cheese; cut into four 1-ounce portions. Roll each into a ball and coat with flour, dredge in egg, and then gently press into pistachios, coating completely. Press each piece into a disk about 1 inch thick. Set medallions on a plate and refrigerate for an hour.

Just before serving, heat the oil in a pan to medium and fry the cheese medallions until the pistachio crust is evenly browned, just under 2 minutes per side. Remove to a plate with a paper towel to drain excess oil.

TO ASSEMBLE:
Quickly toss the baby kale in the vinaigrette until it's lightly coated. Plate the greens, place a medallion on each plate, and garnish with extra chopped mint.

CHEF'S TIP

Substitute the same amount of dried cherries if fresh are not in season. Soak in ¼ cup red wine vinegar for 30 minutes. Drain, discard vinegar, and combine cherries with other ingredients as directed.

Chipotle-Lime Slaw

The combination of spicy chipotle, creamy mayo, and citrus are the perfect addition to the Seared Salmon over Smoked Corn-Quinoa-Black Bean Salsa (recipe page 127) or as a side dish for a classic barbecue.

MAKES 4 CUPS

Ingredients

1 cup mayonnaise

2 cloves garlic, minced

1 teaspoon chipotle chile powder

Juice of 1 lime

1 tablespoon honey

1 teaspoon cumin

½ head green cabbage

4 carrots, peeled

Instructions

In a mixing bowl, whisk mayonnaise, garlic, chipotle, lime juice, honey, and cumin together until it is a smooth aioli.

Finely julienne cabbage and carrots, mix well with chipotle-lime aioli, and refrigerate until ready to serve.

Roasted Garlic Mashed Potatoes

There is an art to making really good mashers. What's important is the subtle garlic flavor, which is accomplished by roasting the garlic beforehand.

SERVES 6

Ingredients

12 medium Yukon potatoes

¾ cup (1½ sticks) unsalted butter

¼ cup heavy cream

¼ cup Roasted Garlic (recipe page 193)

2 tablespoons garlic oil

Salt to taste

2 tablespoons freshly chopped parsley

Instructions

Scrub potatoes to remove traces of dirt. Dice potatoes and put in a pot of water. Boil the potatoes until tender. (Don't boil too long, as they will become watery.)

Meanwhile, in a saucepan melt the butter and add cream, roasted garlic, and garlic oil. Strain the potatoes mash with a potato masher or in an electric mixer with a paddle attachment. Continue to mash potatoes while adding the garlic mixture until mostly smooth. Season with salt to taste and fold in parsley

Parsnip Puree

Light, buttery, and creamy, the neglected and humble parsnip is an interesting alternative to mashed potatoes. Roasted, sautéed, or pureed, this is a vegetable that needs more plate time.

SERVES 4

Ingredients

8 ounces peeled and chopped parsnip

1 cup whole milk

2 tablespoons unsalted butter

Salt to taste

Instructions

In a small saucepan, add parsnips and milk; bring to a boil. Reduce heat and simmer until parsnips are tender. Place parsnips and milk in a blender; add butter and puree until smooth. Salt to taste. Serve with your favorite grilled meat.

Duchesse Potatoes ❄

Traditionally served as elegant rosettes piped from a pastry bag, this extra-rich potato dish has gotten a contemporary makeover by being formed into cylinders for baking. The result is similar in consistency to a twice-baked potato, but with a sleek presentation.

SERVES 8

Ingredients

2 pounds russet potatoes, peeled and cut into 1-inch pieces

Kosher salt and freshly ground black pepper to taste

¼ cup heavy cream

¾ cup (1½ sticks) unsalted butter, divided

2 egg yolks

Instructions

Preheat oven to 400°F. In a large pot, add potatoes and 1 teaspoon kosher salt. Cover with cold water and boil potatoes until fork-tender. Drain the potatoes and then press through a ricer back into the pot for an ultra-smooth rendition of mashed potatoes.

Heat the cream and ¼ cup of the butter in a saucepan over medium-low heat until the butter melts and the cream is warm but not boiling. Stir the mixture into the potatoes. Mix in the egg yolks and season with salt and pepper. Melt another ¼ cup of the butter in a small pot over low heat.

Grease a medium baking dish and the inside of eight stainless steel rings (approximately 2 inches in diameter) with the remaining ¼ cup of butter.

Place the stainless steel rings along the bottom of the prepared baking dish, and with a rubber spatula fill each circle with mashed potatoes. Brush each circle with the melted butter. Bake in the oven until golden brown, 30 to 40 minutes. To serve, use tongs to grip the hot metal rings and a large spoon to press the potato circle onto each plate.

Red Lentil Puree

Montana's Timeless Seeds, Inc. is based in the state's northeastern section, where they grow organic heirloom grains and legumes. The red lentils are smaller and lighter than traditional lentils and have a light, nutty flavor. Served with the Cornish Game Hen Ballotine (recipe page 55), this recipe offers color, texture, and a hearty base to the dish. It is also excellent with duck.

SERVES 6

Ingredients

½ carrot, diced

½ stalk celery, diced

½ small yellow onion, diced

1 bay leaf

2 tablespoons canola or olive oil

1 cup red lentils

1½ cups Chicken Stock (recipe page 184)

Salt to taste

Instructions

Sweat carrot, celery, onion, and bay leaf (mirepoix) in a little canola or olive oil. Add lentils and stock. Simmer until lentils are tender. Remove bay leaf and puree in a food processor. Salt to taste before serving.

Braised Greens for Duck

Serve on top of Herbed White Beans (below) with Duck Grand Marnier Two Ways (recipe page 121).

SERVES 4

Ingredients

1 tablespoon chopped shallot

2 tablespoons canola or olive oil

1 tablespoon chopped garlic

4 cups rough-chopped bitter greens such as chard, collards, or mustard

⅓–½ cup Chicken or Duck Stock (recipes pages 184 and 185)

2 tablespoons apple cider vinegar

Salt to taste

Instructions

Sweat shallots in a little canola or olive oil. Add garlic and sweat as well. Add greens and deglaze with enough stock to simmer in but not so much that it is soupy. When greens are tender and the stock has reduced a bit, add vinegar and salt to taste.

Herbed White Beans

This makes the ideal accompaniment to the Duck Grand Marnier Two Ways (recipe page 121).

SERVES 4

Ingredients

2 tablespoons chopped shallot

2 tablespoons duck fat

2 cups cooked white beans

⅓ cup Duck Stock (recipe page 185)

1 tablespoon chopped fresh parsley

1 tablespoon chopped fresh thyme

Salt to taste

Instructions

Sweat shallots in duck fat. Add beans and deglaze with duck stock. Finish with fresh herbs and salt to taste.

Gorgonzola Au Gratin ☾

Served with the Herb-Crusted Filet Mignon with Port Wine Sauce (recipe page 115), this creamy traditional potato dish is a Chico classic. Prepared with several layers of thin-sliced potatoes and a savory Gorgonzola cheese mixture, it is a versatile complement to meat, poultry, or fish.

SERVES 6

Ingredients

1 large leek, cleaned and sliced thin

1 tablespoon minced garlic

¼ cup chopped raisins

½ cup crumbled Gorgonzola cheese

2 cups heavy whipping cream

1 teaspoon salt

1 teaspoon black pepper

5-6 peeled Idaho potatoes, sliced thin

Instructions

In a saucepan combine leeks, garlic, raisins, Gorgonzola, cream, and salt and pepper; simmer until thick. Remove from heat.

Preheat oven to 350°F. In a greased 9-inch pie pan or decorative baking dish of similar proportion, begin laying potatoes along the bottom of the pan so there is a little overlapping and no surface area showing. Spread a thin coating of the cheese and leek mixture, followed by another layer of potatoes. Press down to squeeze out any air bubbles every few layers. The last layer should be topped with cheese and leek mixture. Cover with aluminum foil and bake for 1 hour, until potatoes are tender (a toothpick or a knife can easily pierce the potatoes). Let cool for 15 minutes before cutting and serving.

Freekeh Fresh

Freekeh is young green wheat that has been toasted and cracked. It's a healthy whole-grain food, much like bulgur wheat, which is high in fiber and serves as a savory substitute for rice and other carbohydrates. It works well with a variety of seafood and poultry dishes.

SERVES 6

Ingredients

1½ cups freekeh

6 cups chicken or vegetable stock

2 tablespoons chopped fresh parsley

Zest from 1 lemon

3 tablespoons olive oil

Salt and freshly ground black pepper to taste

Instructions

Rinse freekeh in cold water. Combine freekeh and stock in a saucepan and bring to a boil. Turn heat down and simmer until freekeh is tender and has soaked up most of the liquid, about 20 minutes. Drain off any excess liquid, then add parsley, lemon zest, and olive oil. Salt and pepper to taste.

Grilled Asparagus

"Less is more" is a maxim that is best applied to the preparation of asparagus. With just the right amount of seasoning and a scant time on the grill, that little hint of grassiness will be drawn out to perfection in this delicate vegetable.

SERVES 6

Ingredients

1 pound asparagus

3 tablespoons olive oil

Sea salt to taste

Instructions

Break the ends off the asparagus. The woody part should naturally snap off where the asparagus is tender. Toss with just enough olive oil to lightly coat. Season with sea salt. Grill until slightly charred and tender.

Roasted Fingerling Potatoes
and Sautéed Kale

Served with Trout Almondine (recipe page 117) or Mustards Pork Chop (recipe page 129), this versatile side dish adds the right amount of heartiness to any dish. The buttery potatoes and bitter kale combine as the perfect canvas for nearly any main course.

SERVES 6

Ingredients

2 pounds fingerling potatoes, halved

¼ cup olive oil

5 tablespoons chopped garlic

¾ cup white wine

3 tablespoons clarified butter

1 head of kale, chopped

Instructions

Preheat oven to 375°F. In a baking dish, coat potatoes in olive oil. Bake until golden brown and crispy, approximately 20 minutes. Keep warm in oven while preparing the trout or pork chop.

In the same pan used to cook the trout, sauté garlic until softened, then add wine and reduce for a few minutes, simmering. For the pork chop or other dish, sauté garlic in 3 tablespoons clarified butter before adding wine. Add kale, coating it with the butter and wine mixture until just wilted. Add roasted fingerlings and toss. Remove from heat and serve with main dish.

Smoked Corn on the Cob

It doesn't take much to elevate the old standby of corn on the cob, whether it's a brush of a homemade sauce or a whole new way of cooking this summer delicacy. The hint of smokiness here adds a layer of flavor that will make this the best corn you've ever tasted.

SERVES 6 (YIELDS ABOUT 2 CUPS KERNELS)

Ingredients

6 ears of corn

2 cups apple wood chips

2 cups ice

Instructions

Remove husks from the corn on the cob. Soak apple wood chips (readily available at a good hardware store or cooking shop) for about an hour. Meanwhile, fire up the grill (yes, even if it's a propane grill), heating coals to 200°F. When the fire comes to the right temperature, spread wood chips evenly over the coals. Place corn in a shallow, heat-safe pan over another pan with ice and put in the smoker or directly on the grill. Close the lid and smoke for 1 hour. The process infuses the essence of the wood into the corn kernels. Serve warm, lathered in Hay Butter (recipe page 187) or with Chico Chimichurri Sauce (recipe page 188). If using for the Smoked Corn-Quinoa-Black Bean Salsa (recipe page 127), remove corn from smoker/grill and let cool. Slice the corn kernels off the cob and reserve for later use; they will last a week in the refrigerator.

SUMMER BLOCK PARTY

CALL IT A HOEDOWN, A SHINDIG, A SOCIAL. We call it the Chico Block Party. Friends and neighbors call it a summer tradition.

Each year in August we circle up the hay bales to form a loose dance floor in the back parking lot of the Saloon. We hoist a food tent, fire up the grills, ice up the drinks, set out the round tables and chairs, and string up the party lights. The venerable local band, Montana Rose, tunes up their guitars and fiddle, while Ms. Claudia William's velvety voice brings it all together. Folks come from three counties to enjoy the music, the dancing, and the simple summer fixin's.

The menu is straightforward: burgers, coleslaw, hot dogs, watermelon, brownies, and sodas. A margarita, maybe? An ice-cold Chico Amber, perhaps? Later a soak in the hot springs to sooth those dance-worn feet? The program is equally forthright: listen, visit, laugh, and dance. The dress code is "come as you are"—the ultimate mix of country folks in their best Wranglers next to river rats fresh from a float on the Yellowstone alongside sundresses and T-shirts. There is no uniform, but western fringe never works so well as when it swings to the rhythm of the music.

The Block Party has grown over twenty years and has become the ultimate celebration of summer. Grab your hat and put on some dancing boots (or river sandals, whatever suits you!) and have some fun!

Main Courses

AT THE HEART OF THE TABLE and the ultimate expression of a "western kitchen" are the main dishes at Chico. Reaching back to classic European roots (think beef Wellington and Grand Marnier duck) as restaurant hallmarks and stretching the boundaries to define "regional" cuisine, we offer contemporary twists on the menu. That means spices, herbs, ingredients, and techniques that range from Asia to Latin America to backyard grilling to a farmer's field that we drive by every day on the way to work.

Note: Recipes denoted by are Chico "Classics."

CHEF'S TIP

For elegant small plates, the beef
Wellington can be prepared as
individual 2-ounce portions to
make eight servings. To adapt the
recipe, sear the whole tenderloin as
directed and let cool. Once it is cool,
cut meat into 2-ounce squares. Cut
puff pastry into eight 4-inch squares
(this may require a second sheet)
and wrap each piece of meat individually. Bake at the same temperature
for 20 to 25 minutes, monitoring
with a meat thermometer.

Beef Wellington ✺

This traditional English recipe is an elegant and decadent dinner. Beef tenderloin is layered with earthy duxelles, then wrapped in a buttery puff pastry, and is so rich that it barely needs accoutrements. In Chico's historic dining room, this signature dish is prepared for two, carved tableside, and served with au jus.

SERVES 4

Ingredients

FOR THE BEEF:

1 pound beef tenderloin, trimmed

½ tablespoon sea salt

1 tablespoon black pepper

1 tablespoon canola oil, plus more for coating baking pan

FOR THE DUXELLES:

2 tablespoons unsalted butter

2 tablespoons finely diced shallot

2 cloves garlic, minced

1 cup finely diced cremini mushrooms

½ cup white wine

FOR THE PASTRY:

1 (10 x 15-inch) puff pastry sheet, thawed

1 egg

Instructions

TO PREPARE THE BEEF TENDERLOIN:

Trim the fat and muscle off each tenderloin unless your butcher has already done so. Season the trimmed tenderloin with salt and pepper. Heat oil in a large skillet over high heat until almost smoking; sear meat until brown on all sides. Remove from pan and let cool.

Preheat oven to 375°F. Coat a baking pan with oil and set aside.

TO PREPARE THE DUXELLES:

Duxelles are a French mixture of lightly sautéed mushrooms and aromatics. In a medium sauté pan melt butter and sweat with shallots and garlic. Add mushrooms and sweat as well. Add wine and simmer over low heat until liquid is almost completely reduced. Let cool.

TO PREPARE THE WELLINGTON:

Lay puff pastry sheet on a clean, flat surface. Spread the duxelles in the center of the pastry in an area that is the same size as the tenderloin. Place meat on top of the duxelles. Fold in sides of pastry to enclose tenderloin like a present. Tuck the corners of the pastry inside, smoothly pressed against the meat. Set on the oiled baking pan, fold-side down.

Crack the egg in a bowl and whisk with a fork. Brush egg wash over the pastry. Place in the preheated oven and bake for 30 to 40 minutes for medium rare. Use a meat thermometer to check temperature; puff pastry should be golden brown when done. Remember that the pastry-wrapped meat will continue to cook even after it is removed from the oven, so it's best to undercook by about 5°F.

When Wellington is cooked to desired temperature, remove from the oven and let rest for 10 to 15 minutes. Slice into four portions and serve with Duchesse Potatoes (recipe page 89), grilled asparagus, or your favorite side dishes.

CHEF'S TIP

This recipe is represented as an entree here, but it can easily be pre-pared as an appetizer by cutting the halibut fillets into smaller 3-ounce pieces to serve eight people. When cooking smaller pieces, be careful not to crowd the pieces in the pan during browning. Reduce oven time, baking 5 to 8 minutes instead.

Pine Nut–Crusted Halibut ✺
with Port Wine Butter Sauce and Mango Salsa

This longtime favorite is a famous example of Chico's style of "layering" flavors. Here, with fresh halibut flown in twice a week, we offset the flaky white fish with a heavy coating of pine nuts and a deep buttery sauce. A crisp fruit salsa lightens up the ensemble. Traditionally we splurge on mango, but other seasonal fruits are an acceptable substitute. Strawberries and melons work nicely too. This recipe also works with other firm, white fish, such as sole. The port wine butter sauce cannot be reheated or chilled, so prepare it while the halibut is in the oven or just before serving.

SERVES 4 (MAKES 2 CUPS MANGO SALSA)

Ingredients

FOR THE PINE NUT CRUST:

2 cups pine nuts

¾ cup bread crumbs

1 teaspoon salt

⅓ cup parsley

FOR THE HALIBUT:

½ cup all-purpose flour

1 cup buttermilk

4 (6-ounce) halibut fillets

1 teaspoon olive oil

FOR THE PORT WINE BUTTER SAUCE:

2 cups port wine

½ cup heavy whipping cream

½ cup (1 stick) unsalted butter

FOR THE MANGO SALSA:

1 mango, peeled, seeded, and diced

½ small red onion, diced

½ red bell pepper, diced

½ cup chopped chives

3 tablespoons raspberry vinegar

2 tablespoons honey

2 tablespoons chopped cilantro

Instructions

TO PREPARE THE PINE NUT CRUST:

In a food processor combine all ingredients. Pulse until nuts are diced, but not too finely; remove and set aside. You can also prepare the crust by hand. Be sure to dice the nuts before combining with the other ingredients.

TO PREPARE THE HALIBUT:

Preheat oven to 400°F. Place flour, buttermilk, and pine nut mixture in separate bowls and arrange in a line on the counter. Take fillets and dip one side only in flour, then buttermilk, then pine nuts. On the stove heat a pan with 1 teaspoon olive oil and, with crust-side down, sauté the fish until crust mixture is golden brown. Place the sautéed fish on a greased baking dish, bare fish-side down and bake in the oven for 8 to 10 minutes.

TO PREPARE THE PORT WINE BUTTER SAUCE:

This sauce cannot be reheated or chilled, so prepare it while the main course is in the oven or just before serving. Reduce port over medium heat until it forms a syrup and coats a metal spoon, about 20 minutes. Add cream and reduce until thick. Remove from heat and add butter, stirring constantly until butter is melted and sauce is smooth. Turn heat down to low and use promptly.

TO MAKE THE MANGO SALSA:

Mix all ingredients in a bowl and refrigerate until needed.

TO PLATE:

Serve the halibut in a pool of port wine butter sauce, topped with the fresh mango salsa.

Pistachio-Crusted Rack of Lamb

Bringing the offerings of local ranches to the table, here the gamey flavors of lamb epitomize Montana's grassy foothills. Paired with a medley of herbs and pistachios, the meat is encrusted in a crunch that enhances the juicy tenderness of this entree.

SERVES 4–8

Ingredients

2 tablespoons canola

1½-pound rack of lamb

½ cup panko bread crumbs

½ cup chopped pistachios

½ teaspoon chopped fresh rosemary

2 tablespoons chopped fresh parsley

1 teaspoon chopped fresh sage

1 tablespoon chopped fresh thyme

2 tablespoons Dijon mustard

Instructions

In a cast-iron skillet or heavy-bottomed pan with heated canola oil, sear lamb and let cool. Combine panko and pistachios with herbs. Rub lamb with mustard, then dip into pistachio-panko mixture, pressing on all sides to form a crust. Bake at 375°F for 30 to 40 minutes, depending on the size of the rack, for medium temperature. Remove from the oven and let the rack rest on a cutting board for 10 minutes to seal in the cooking juices. Slice and serve with your choice of savory sides. This would pair well with Roasted Fingerling Potatoes and Sautéed Kale (recipe page 95).

CHEF'S TIP

Be cautious not to add too much salt to the veloute sauce since the brined chicken is already saturated with the ideal amount of salt.

Pan-Roasted Chicken
with Herbed Veloute Sauce

This is not your plain-old Wednesday night chicken dinner! The process of brining, searing, and roasting creates the crispiest skin paired with meat that is moist and packed with tangy flavor. Take the time to make the veloute sauce and you will be creating an unforgettable chicken dinner. For best results, brine chicken and make the stock one day ahead.

SERVES 2-4

Ingredients

FOR THE CHICKEN AND BRINE:

4 cups water

2 bay leaves

1 tablespoon peppercorns

1 lemon, halved

⅓ cup kosher salt

1½ tablespoons fresh thyme

½ fresh rosemary sprig

1½ tablespoons fresh parsley

4 shallots, quartered

4 cloves garlic, smashed

2 cups ice

1 roasting chicken

FOR THE HERBED VELOUTE SAUCE:

1 tablespoon olive oil

1½ cups julienned leeks

4 tablespoons unsalted butter

½ cup all-purpose flour

4 cups chicken stock

1 tablespoon minced fresh parsley

1 tablespoon minced fresh Instructions

thyme

1 teaspoon minced fresh sage

½ teaspoon minced fresh rosemary

1 tablespoon lemon juice

Pinch of salt

Instructions

TO BRINE THE CHICKEN:

Put all ingredients, except ice and chicken, in a saucepan and bring to a boil. Simmer for 5 to 10 minutes. Remove from heat and add ice. Put in the refrigerator to cool.

Meanwhile, break down a whole fryer chicken by removing the breasts and deboning the thighs, keeping drumsticks and skin intact. Place the chicken pieces in the cooled brine; keep submersed 6 hours or overnight. Reserve wings, carcass, and giblets to make Chicken Stock (recipe page 184).

TO MAKE THE HERBED VELOUTE SAUCE:

In a saucepan over medium-low heat, sweat leeks in olive oil. In a separate pan, melt butter and whisk in flour to make a roux. When leeks are translucent, add chicken stock and bring to a boil. Whisk in roux thoroughly to eliminate any lumps. Reduce heat to a simmer. Simmer until thickened. Add herbs, lemon juice, and a pinch of salt.

TO ROAST THE CHICKEN:

Preheat oven to 350°F.

Remove breasts, thighs, and drumsticks from brine. Rinse and pat dry.

Heat a large cast-iron skillet over medium-high heat, adding just enough canola oil to cover the bottom. When pan is hot, add chicken skin-side down, one piece at a time, to keep the pan temperature consistent. Sear until skin is crispy and golden brown. Remove and place on a plate to hold until all chicken is seared. You may need to add more oil between searing; allow the pan oil to heat again before cooking another piece of chicken. Turn the pieces over and place skin-side up in the skillet. Roast in the oven for around 15 minutes until chicken is cooked through.

Serve with herbed veloute sauce and your favorite seasonal accompaniments.

Herb-Crusted Filet Mignon 🍋
with Port Wine Sauce

Montana is famous for its beef, and Chico uses certified Angus cuts for slice-like-butter tenderness. The combination of herbs in this recipe brings out the natural, rich flavors of the filet, while the sauce deepens the savory result.

SERVES 4 (MAKES APPROXIMATELY 1 CUP SAUCE)

Ingredients

FOR THE PORT WINE SAUCE:

1½ cups port wine

1 cup sweet vermouth

½ cup granulated sugar

FOR THE STEAKS:

¼ cup fennel seeds

¼ cup whole coriander seeds

1 teaspoon salt

1 teaspoon black pepper

4 (8-ounce) beef tenderloin steaks

4 tablespoons crumbled Gorgonzola cheese

Instructions

TO MAKE THE PORT WINE SAUCE:

Combine ingredients in a small saucepan. Reduce over medium heat until the mixture forms a syrup, about 30 minutes. When it coats a spoon, the sauce is done. It can be made the day before and will keep in the refrigerator for up to a week. Warm over low heat when ready to serve.

TO MAKE THE STEAKS:

In a spice grinder or blender, pulse fennel and coriander seeds, salt, and pepper until coarsely ground. Roll outer edge of each steak in herbs to form a crust; do not encrust cut ends. Grill each steak to desired temperature.

TO PLATE:

Warm port wine sauce in a saucepan. Ladle warm sauce onto individual serving plates, making a small pool slightly larger than the steaks; set the steaks on top of the sauce. Top with Gorgonzola cheese crumbles.

CHEF'S TIP
GRILLING RECOMMENDATIONS

- Rare   2 to 4 minutes on each side
- Medium rare   6 to 8 minutes on each side
- Medium   10 to 12 minutes on each side
- Medium well   14 to 18 minutes on each side

Trout Almondine

Locally caught trout benefits from the simple preparation and nutty crust of this recipe. It goes well with the Roasted Fingerling Potatoes and Sautéed Kale (recipe page 95). To serve, place the potato mixture in the middle of each plate, top with one or two sides of trout, and drizzle with remaining clarified butter.

SERVES 4–8

Ingredients

2 cups panko bread crumbs

1 cup almond slices

8 sides of trout (4 fish), deboned with skin on

1 cup clarified butter, divided

Instructions

For the crust, combine panko and almonds in a shallow bowl. Press trout fillets to coat each side for the breading. In a large sauté pan or cast-iron skillet, add 2 tablespoons of clarified butter and warm over medium heat. Cooking two pieces at a time, place trout skin-side down and brown for 3 to 4 minutes, then flip and cook the other side for another 3 to 4 minutes until crust is toasty brown and fish is flaky. Remove from the pan and set aside on a warmed plate. Repeat with remaining sides of trout, adding more butter each time.

Hold in a warm oven while preparing kale and roasted potatoes.

Farro Risotto
with Shaved Brussels Sprouts and Pancetta

Farro is an ancient relative of wheat, and the heirloom grain is still favored in Italy for its chewy texture and rich, nutty flavor. Our farro is Montana grown by Timeless Seeds, Inc. This dish takes about twenty minutes to cook at a simmer and makes a great vegetarian entree without the pancetta and with the substitution of vegetable stock.

SERVES 6

Ingredients

¼ cup diced shallot

1 tablespoon canola oil

3 cups farro (semi-pearled variety)

1 cup white wine

2 cups chicken or vegetable stock

2 tablespoons unsalted butter

Salt to taste

4 cups brussels sprouts

1¼ cups diced pancetta (optional)

¼ cup apple cider vinegar

Instructions

Sweat shallots in 1 tablespoon canola oil. Add farro and deglaze with white wine. Simmer over low heat, stirring often. Add chicken or vegetable stock a little at a time as the farro hydrates. Cooking time is approximately 20 minutes. Finish with butter and salt to taste.

Trim stems from brussels sprouts and shave thin slices on a mandoline or food processor. In a skillet, render the pancetta over low heat until crisp. Add a little canola if needed, then turn up heat to medium high. Add brussels sprouts and quickly caramelize, being careful not to overcook. Deglaze with cider vinegar, then add salt to taste. Brussels should be al dente.

To serve, spoon cooked farro into shallow bowls and top with brussels sprouts and pancetta.

Duck Grand Marnier Two Ways

During the mid-1970s Chef Larry Edwards perfected a Duck L'Orange that became a staple of the Chico menu. With a twist and a nod to this dish's French origins, Chef Dave Wells improved this classic with a preparation of the duck in two different ways: confit and a crisply seared breast. The most challenging aspect of this recipe is the Grand Marnier sauce; it requires several hours to prepare. Make the sauce one or two days in advance for best results.

SERVES 4

Ingredients

FOR THE DUCK:

1 whole Pekin duck

4 celery stalks

2 medium-large carrots, peeled

2 large onions

1 tablespoon tomato paste

Bouquet garni (1 sprig fresh sage, 2 bay leaves and 3 sprigs fresh thyme wrapped in kitchen string)

1 tablespoon chopped fresh thyme

1 tablespoon chopped fresh parsley

1 cup kosher salt

1¼ teaspoons juniper berries, ground

1 cup rendered duck fat

6 thyme sprigs

4 parsley sprigs

2 cloves garlic

FOR THE GRAND MARNIER SAUCE:

2 quarts Duck Stock (recipe page 185)

¼ cup Grand Marnier liqueur

Zest and juice from 1 orange

Salt to taste

Instructions

TO PREPARE THE DUCK:

Start by breaking the carcass down. Remove the breasts and legs, then trim the carcass of all fat. Place fat in a saucepan and render over low heat. Trim the carcass of all excess meat; reserve for later use. (Be thorough, as the trim from this can be used for the Cornish Game Hen Ballotine recipe, page 55; freeze if desired).

Preheat oven to 400°F. To make a mirepoix, rough chop celery and carrots, quarter the onions, and rub with tomato paste. Place mirepoix on a sheet pan along with the duck carcass. Roast in the oven until browned. Place mirepoix and duck carcass in a stockpot and cover with cold water. Add bouquet garni and bring to a boil, then lower heat so water is barely simmering. Let simmer for 8 hours or overnight. Strain and reserve. This should yield about 1 gallon (4 quarts).

TO MAKE THE GRAND MARNIER SAUCE:

In a saucepan bring 2 quarts duck stock to a boil. Lower heat to a simmer. Let reduce slowly while skimming any impurities that float to the surface. Reduce to around 2 cups. Add Grand Marnier and zest and juice from the orange and reduce until sauce coats the back of a spoon. Salt to taste. This can be made the day before and refrigerated until ready to serve; warm over medium-low heat.

TO PREPARE THE CONFIT LEGS:

Mix the chopped herbs with the kosher salt and 1 teaspoon of ground juniper berries. Rub the duck legs with 2 tablespoons of the herb salt. Cover and place in the refrigerator for 8 hours.

Remove duck from refrigerator, rinse legs with water, and pat dry. Place legs in a baking dish just big enough to hold them both. Cover with rendered duck fat. Add thyme and parsley sprigs, remaining juniper berries, and garlic cloves. Cover and bake in a 250°F oven for 4 to 6 hours until tender. Let cool in fat and reserve. This can also be made a day ahead.

TO COOK THE DUCK BREAST AND SERVE:

Heat a pan over medium heat. Score the fat on the duck breasts, season with salt and place in pan skin-side down. Let fat render until the skin is crispy. Turn breasts over and sear. Cook to medium rare. Remove from pan and let rest for 10 minutes.

Meanwhile, add confit legs to the pan and sear until skin is crispy. Turn legs over and put in a 400°F oven until warmed through.

Slice breasts and serve with legs over Herbed White Beans (recipe page 91) with Braised Greens for Duck (recipe page 91). Drizzle with Grand Marnier sauce and enjoy.

Seared Halibut
with Citrus-Coconut Broth and Carrot-Snap Pea Salad over Ginger-Scallion Basmati Rice

The silky richness of coconut and the brightness of citrus in the sauce showcase the flaky, mild flavor of the halibut in Chef Dave Wells's Thai-influenced fresh catch. The rice is a canvas for all the flavors, and the accent of a small garden salad adds the perfect amount of crisp texture.

SERVES 6

Ingredients

FOR THE CITRUS-COCONUT BROTH:

¼ cup diced shallot

3 cloves garlic, diced

1 teaspoon red curry paste

½ cup chopped lemongrass

3 cups coconut milk

Zest and juice of 1 lemon

Zest and juice of 1 lime

1 teaspoon fish sauce

1 teaspoon crushed red pepper flakes

1 tablespoon grated fresh ginger

FOR THE GINGER-SCALLION RICE:

3 cups basmati rice

4½ cups water

1 cup thinly sliced scallion

¼ cup minced fresh ginger

2 tablespoons mirin

½ teaspoon sesame oil

¼ cup tamari

1 teaspoon fish sauce

FOR THE CARROT AND SNAP PEA SALAD:

1 large carrot, peeled

1 cup snap peas

1 teaspoon tamari

1 teaspoon rice vinegar

FOR THE FISH:

2 tablespoons canola oil

2 pounds fresh halibut, cut into 6-ounce fillets

Instructions

TO MAKE THE CITRUS-COCONUT BROTH:

In a saucepan sweat shallots and garlic. Add curry paste. Stir and cook until fragrant. Add the remaining ingredients and reduce by a third. Strain through a fine-mesh sieve and keep warm in the saucepan until ready to serve.

TO MAKE THE GINGER-SCALLION RICE:

Rinse the rice well in cold water. Place in a saucepan with 4½ cups water. Bring to a boil, cover, and reduce to low heat. Cook for 15 minutes. While rice is cooking, in a mixing bowl add the scallions, ginger, mirin, sesame oil, tamari, and fish sauce and whisk until well combined. When rice is done, cover with a tea towel and let rest for 5 minutes. Fluff with a fork and fold in the scallion-ginger mixture.

TO ASSEMBLE THE SALAD:

Very finely julienne carrots and snap peas. Dress with tamari and rice vinegar. Set aside.

TO MAKE THE FISH:

Heat a large, oven-safe pan with canola oil over medium-high heat until it just begins to smoke. Add halibut to the pan and sear on one side, approximately 3 minutes depending on thickness of the fillets. Leave the fish in the pan and transfer it to a 350°F oven; cook until internal temperature is 140°F, approximately 5 minutes. Remove from oven.

TO ASSEMBLE THE DISH:

Spoon rice into a bowl and top with cooked halibut. Garnish the halibut generously with carrot-snap pea salad. Finally, pour a little citrus-coconut broth into a bowl and serve alongside the fish.

Orecchiette Pasta with Blistered Cherry Tomatoes and Carrot-Top Pesto

In the Chico greenhouse, head gardener Jeannie Duran cultivates at least five different varieties of little tomatoes—Little Gems, Sungolds, Cherry, Grape, and Pear. The ideal humid environment of the geothermally heated greenhouse produces a forest of tomato plants that grow to the ceiling and offer up a burst of color and flavor that is best consumed right off the vines. But next best is a quick-blistered version tossed with pasta and Chef David Wells's carrot-top pesto.

SERVES 6

Ingredients

FOR THE CARROT-TOP PESTO:

2 cups packed carrot tops, stemmed

2 small cloves garlic

½ cup pine nuts

½ cup grated Parmesan cheese

4 tablespoons fresh lemon juice

Zest of 1 lemon

1½ cups olive oil

Salt and freshly ground black pepper to taste

FOR THE PASTA:

1 pound dry orecchiette pasta

8 cups salted water

FOR THE TOMATOES:

1 tablespoon olive oil

1 teaspoon minced garlic

3 cups grape or cherry or other small tomato variety

½ teaspoon kosher salt

1 teaspoon unsalted butter

Instructions

TO MAKE THE CARROT-TOP PESTO:

Place carrot tops, garlic, pine nuts, Parmesan, lemon juice, and lemon zest in a food processor or blender and combine until all ingredients are roughly chopped. Spoon into a bowl and fold in olive oil (if you process the oil, it becomes bitter) until well blended. Season with salt and pepper to taste.

TO MAKE THE PASTA:

Prepare orecchiette pasta by boiling salted water and cooking until al dente. Remove from heat, drain, and toss with pesto. Cover and set aside.

TO MAKE THE TOMATOES:

Heat the oil and garlic in a cast-iron skillet or heavy sauté pan over high heat until garlic is just softened, but not brown.

Carefully add the tomatoes and cook undisturbed for 1 minute. Stir gently and cook for another minute. Mix again and cook for 1 more minute, each time allowing the tomatoes to char or brown a bit and blister, but not break apart.

Remove the pan from the heat, gently toss with the salt and butter until the tomatoes are evenly coated.

TO SERVE:

Divide orecchiette with pesto into bowls, top with warm tomatoes, and serve immediately.

Seared Salmon over Smoked Corn-Quinoa-Black Bean Salsa with Charred Scallion Crema

Layers of spice from the salsa and a touch of citrus from the Chipotle-Lime Slaw (recipe page 86) balance the oily fish, while the cream sauce adds a cooling finish to the palate.

SERVES 6 (MAKES 1 CUP CREMA)

Ingredients

FOR THE CHARRED SCALLION CREMA:

5 scallions

1 cup sour cream

FOR THE SALSA:

1½ tablespoons cumin

1½ tablespoons coriander

1 cup Smoked Corn on the Cob (recipe page 97)

2 cups cooked black beans

1 cup cooked quinoa

¼ cup chopped cilantro

½ red onion, fine diced

1 jalapeño, diced

⅓ cup apple cider vinegar

⅓ cup olive oil

FOR THE FISH:

2 tablespoons canola oil

6 (5-ounce) fresh Ora Salmon or wild king salmon fillets

Instructions

TO PREPARE THE CHARRED SCALLION CREMA:
Trim the ends off scallions. Using either a grill or a broiler, blacken the outer layer to a perfect char. Remove from heat and allow to cool. Once cool, finely chop scallions and mix with sour cream in a blender until smooth.

TO MAKE THE SALSA:
In a small pan over medium heat, toast the cumin and coriander. Let cool and grind in a spice grinder. Combine ground cumin and coriander with smoked corn, black beans, and cooked quinoa; mix well. Add cilantro, onions, jalapeño, vinegar, and oil, mixing again, and refrigerate until later.

TO COOK THE SALMON:
In a large sauté pan, heat canola over medium-high until barely smoking. Carefully add salmon and sear fillets for 3 minutes. Flip fillets and cook another 3 minutes until both sides are crisp, but barely browned.

TO SERVE:
Spoon approximately ¾ cup salsa onto individual plates and top with a seared salmon fillet, then garnish with a heaping spoonful of Chipotle-Lime Slaw (recipe page 86) and drizzle with charred scallion crema.

Mustards Pork Chop

Inspired by Napa Valley's famous Mustards Grill, the sweet, spicy, and caramelized elements of this hearty meal have become a Montana favorite at Chico. Grilling over low coals on the barbecue until the outside of the pork is perfectly charred (not burnt to bitter) is the secret to success.

SERVES 6

CHEF'S TIP

At Chico we use the sous vide method to prepare this thick-cut pork to the perfect and consistent medium temperature. At home, for even cooking, place your chops in a sealable plastic bag with a sprinkle of water inside to keep the bag from tearing and pound slightly with the smooth side of a meat mallet so that the thickness of each cut of meat is even. Marinate in the bag overnight if desired.

Ingredients

FOR THE PORK:

6 (10-ounce) center cut, bone-in pork chops, frenched

FOR THE MARINADE:

1 cup hoisin sauce (a Chinese black bean sauce; Lee Kum Kee is a reliable brand, but any premade option will work)

1 tablespoon brown sugar

1½ tablespoons tamari soy sauce

1½ tablespoons sherry

1½ tablespoons rice vinegar

1 scallion, minced

1 teaspoon Tabasco

1½ teaspoons minced peeled fresh ginger

1½ teaspoons minced garlic

¾ teaspoon freshly ground white pepper

¼ cup minced fresh cilantro leaves and stems

1 tablespoon sesame oil

FOR THE MUSTARD SAUCE:

½ cup granulated sugar

¼ cup mustard powder (such as Colman's)

2 egg yolks

½ cup red wine vinegar

¾ cup crème fraîche or sour cream

Instructions

TO PREPARE THE PORK CHOPS:

To "french" the pork chops, trim the excess fat from the rib bones, leaving them exposed. Slightly tenderize the meat with a mallet to an even 1-inch thickness. Refrigerate and set aside.

TO MAKE THE MARINADE:

Combine all the ingredients in a bowl and mix well. Coat pork chops evenly and marinate for 3 hours or overnight in the refrigerator.

TO MAKE THE MUSTARD SAUCE:

Whisk sugar and mustard together in a metal mixing bowl. Place over a double boiler, whisking in egg yolks and vinegar. Cook over the simmering water for 10 to 15 minutes, stirring occasionally, until thickened. Remove from heat and allow the mixture to cool to room temperature. When cool, gently fold in the crème fraîche. The sauce can be kept refrigerated for 2 days before serving.

TO COOK:

Place the chops on a barbecue with coals settled to a medium heat/flame and grill for 5 minutes on each side for a medium temperature (139°F on a meat thermometer) or 8 minutes on each side for medium well. Brush excess marinade onto pork while grilling to enhance the caramelized flavors.

TO SERVE:

In the restaurant, the pork chop is served over Roasted Fingerling Potatoes and Sautéed Kale (recipe page 95) with a drizzle of the mustard sauce.

Yellowstone Grass-Fed Beef Flat Iron Steak with Hay Butter

Hay butter, hay butter, hay butter! This is a real thing at Chico and quite likely invented by Chef Dave Wells, who brings out the tongue-in-cheek essence of Montana beef that was raised eating grass with this unforgettable hay-infused clarified butter that conjures summer and fresh-cut fields with every bite. It tastes like grass, but in a good way. Try it!

SERVES 4

Ingredients

FOR THE MARINADE:

¼ cup apple cider vinegar

2 tablespoons olive oil

3 large cloves garlic, minced

2 teaspoons Dijon mustard

2 teaspoons chopped fresh oregano

2 teaspoons Worcestershire sauce

2 teaspoons coarsely ground black pepper

FOR THE STEAK:

3 pounds flat iron steak (flank steak or hangar steak are acceptable substitutes)

Nonstick vegetable oil spray

1 cup Hay Butter (recipe page 187)

Instructions

TO MARINATE THE STEAK:

Combine the marinade ingredients in a large, nonreactive bowl. Place steak in the bowl and turn so that it is completely coated with the marinade. Chill and marinate for at least 2 hours and up to overnight.

TO GRILL THE STEAK:

Prepare barbecue (medium-high heat) or a cast-iron skillet sprayed with nonstick vegetable oil spray on the stovetop. Remove meat from marinade; discard marinade. Grill steak to desired doneness, about 4 minutes per side for medium rare.

When the steak has cooked to your preferred level of doneness, remove from the grill and place on a cutting board. Cover with aluminum foil to hold in the heat while the steak rests for 10 to 15 minutes.

TO SERVE:

Cut meat across the grain. Flat iron, flank, and hangar steaks can be tough and chewy unless you cut it in a way that breaks up the muscle fibers. So cut the steak at a sharp diagonal into thin slices. Liberally spoon hay butter over the top of the meat. Add a salad or sides of your choice, and serve with a little more of the hay butter for drizzling.

Pasty in Paradise

The pasty is a legacy from Cornish miners who immigrated to Butte, Montana, during the Copper King era. This homey meat pie is served as a casual meal in the Saloon and pairs nicely with a locally brewed Chico Amber.

SERVES 4

Ingredients

FOR THE CRUST:

1 batch Pie Dough, (recipe page 191)

1 egg, beaten

FOR THE FILLING:

2 tablespoons canola oil

1 small yellow onion, diced

1 large carrot, peeled and diced

1 rib celery, diced

1 tablespoon fresh thyme

4 cups cubed beef tenderloin

1 cup cubed fingerling potatoes

1 teaspoon kosher salt

¼ teaspoon black pepper

Instructions

Prepare Pie Dough (recipe page 191) and chill for an hour.

Meanwhile, in a skillet heat canola oil over medium. Sweat onion, carrots, celery, and thyme (mirepoix). When mirepoix is softened, add beef and potatoes. Cook until meat is lightly browned on all sides; add salt and pepper. Remove from heat and set aside to cool.

Preheat oven to 350°F. Divide the dough into four equal balls. On a lightly floured surface, roll each ball into a round about ¼ inch thick. Spoon beef and potato mixture into the center of the dough round, then fold pastry in half, tuck the top edge under the bottom edge, and seal by pressing with your fingers or marking with a fork. Repeat with all four rounds, then place on a buttered sheet pan. Brush liberally with the egg wash and bake for 45 minutes to 1 hour, until golden brown.

Serve warm with Mixed Greens with Orange-Ginger Vinaigrette (recipe page 84).

Herb-Crusted Prime Rib ☀

The most-ordered item on the Chico menu is afforded a striking presence on the plate with the bone-in effect that suggests a special occasion. The salty herb crust accents the marbled meat with savory goodness and cements this as a perennial favorite.

SERVES 8

Ingredients

1 bone-in prime rib

2 tablespoons olive oil

¼ cup kosher salt

½ cup chopped fresh parsley

¼ cup chopped fresh thyme

⅛ cup chopped fresh rosemary

⅛ cup chopped fresh sage

¼ cup chopped garlic

Instructions

Preheat oven to 450°F. Rub the prime rib with olive oil and season generously with kosher salt. Roast prime rib for 15 minutes, until golden brown. Take out of the oven and let cool to room temperature.

Mix herbs and garlic together and rub on prime rib. Set oven to 250°F. Roast prime rib another 2 hours, depending on the size, until it reaches an internal temperature of 120°F. Remove from the oven and let rest. The residual cooking while resting should bring the prime rib up to medium rare. For rare pull the prime rib at 110°F.

Slice and serve with Roasted Garlic Mashed Potatoes (recipe page 87) and Grilled Asparagus (recipe page 94).

HARVEST DINNER

WHEN PARADISE VALLEY FADES FROM GREEN TO YELLOW and then to wind-drift blonde, it's clear that autumn has settled in. Fall's warm days often linger into Thanksgiving, when the relief of the harvest calls for celebration. Whether that's a collection of twenty people or just two, there's a dinner table set at Chico. Our waitstaff stands at the ready, sharing both a classic menu and the freshness of daily specials.

The Wine Cellar is a favorite private dining area for guests. Housed in an original stone building that dates back to 1897, it once enclosed the hotel's electrical generator. Now there is a long, handmade dinner table that seats exactly eighteen people. Tucked behind the historic main lodge, the building embodies the best of what makes Chico distinct—rustic architecture combined with an elegant approach to service and cuisine.

While the main restaurant bustles with groups and couples, the privacy of the Wine Cellar offers a relaxing escape from the hubbub. In here, candlelight and music bounces off the wood and stone, while a team of servers presents preparations of lamb and game hen. Accents of wild sage, antlers, and leather in the table setting hint at the season. The wine is selected from a collection of over three thousand bottles and flows generously.

Entertaining at Chico often translates to casual sophistication. No jacket and tie is needed, formal attire isn't a prerequisite, and there is such a thing as "nice" jeans. In contrast, the quality of the service and the seasonal offerings err on the side of refinement with the hope of providing an experience that's approachable, delicious, and memorable.

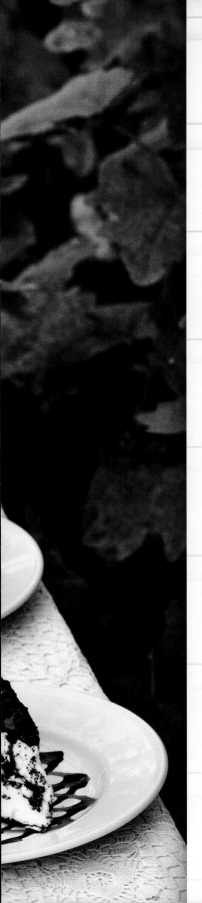

Desserts

IF LIVING LIFE WELL MEANS STARTING WITH DESSERT FIRST, then you've turned to the right chapter!

In the historic dining room, dessert is the first thing that guests see when they walk through the door. The dessert cart displays the evening's selection and makes a welcome, and rather obvious, suggestion that a sweet splurge is on the menu. The assortment of sweets in this chapter offers a splendid array of relatively easy yet impressive items worth mastering. At one end of the spectrum, there is the finesse required for the pâte brisée pastry in the Black Truffle Chocolate Tart with Port-Infused Flathead Cherries, and on the opposite end, the fantastically simple Grand Marnier Crème Brûlée. Both are delectable and wildly different. That's reason enough for the dessert-first mantra.

Note: Recipes denoted by are Chico "Classics."

Flaming Orange ☀

Served since the late 1970s, this dramatic dessert is an original recipe from Chef Larry Edwards. It is a creative combination of whimsy and wildness, the childhood experience of a Creamsicle partnered with a fascination for fire. The result is a pleasing concoction that elevates ice cream to new heights. When preparing this flashy dessert, it is essential that you use high-quality ice cream; Chico uses locally made Wilcoxson's from Livingston.

SERVES 8

Ingredients

FOR THE ORANGES:

8 large oranges

10 ounces bittersweet chocolate

FOR THE FILLING:

4 cups high-quality vanilla ice cream (Wilcoxson's is made right in Livingston)

½ ounce Grand Marnier

½ ounce Triple Sec

½ ounce vodka

½ cup sour cream

1 ounce frozen orange juice concentrate, thawed

FOR THE MERINGUE TOPPING:

4 egg whites, room temperature

¼ teaspoon cream of tartar

¾ cup granulated sugar

¼ teaspoon almond extract

FOR THE FLAMBÉ:

8 ounces 151 rum

Instructions

TO PREPARE THE ORANGES:

Cut the tops and bottoms from the oranges, making the top cut about a ¼-inch slice and the bottom about a ½-inch slice. Save the bottom slice. Hollow out each orange by running a grapefruit spoon halfway between the skin and the pulp on the top, leaving only the rind as a kind of shell for the filling. The inside of the oranges should be clean of any pulp. Set the remaining bottom slice of rind inside the shell to act as a stopper for the filling (must also be cleaned of pulp). Set aside.

Melt bittersweet chocolate in a double boiler over medium heat. Using a small ladle, spoon melted chocolate inside orange rind; with a soup spoon smear it until all white surfaces are coated. Repeat with each orange, then place oranges into a baking dish and freeze until chocolate has hardened (about an hour).

TO PREPARE THE FILLING:

Let ice cream soften slightly so that it is easy to scoop but not runny. Place in the bowl of an electric mixer fitted with a dough hook. If mixing by hand, use a stiff plastic spatula. Add remaining ingredients, then mix or stir until it is the consistency of a thick milkshake. Remove chocolate-lined oranges from the freezer and fill with the ice cream mixture, being careful not to overfill. Return oranges to freezer for about an hour.

TO PREPARE THE MERINGUE TOPPING:

Whip egg whites with cream of tartar until soft peaks form. Slowly add the sugar a little at a time until stiff peaks form; add almond extract. Using a pastry bag with a rosette tip, pipe domes of meringue on the frozen oranges and return them to the freezer.

TO ASSEMBLE:

When ready to serve, remove oranges from freezer and let stand for 15 minutes at room temperature. Warm eight heat-safe plates in a 400°F oven for about 5 minutes. Place on another cool plate for serving, then place oranges on hot plates. Pour 1 ounce of rum over the top of each orange and bring the dessert to the table. Carefully light with a match. The flambé will brown the meringue while softening the ice cream and chocolate inside. Let the flame burn out entirely before taking the first bite!

Mixed Berry Cobbler
with Shortbread Topping

The lazy cook's pie, a cobbler is a quick dessert that is a standard offering at Chico because its buttery warm pastry pairs perfectly with any seasonal fruit, from mixed berries to prized Montana huckleberrys or a fleeting crop of peaches from nearby Washington state. When served warm, topped with ice cream, who could resist a piece?

SERVES 8

Ingredients

FOR THE FILLING:

½ cup water

½ cup port or sweet red wine

2 pounds (32 ounces) fresh or frozen mixed berries, such as strawberries, blackberries, blueberries, raspberries

½ cup granulated sugar

1 teaspoon ground cinnamon

2 tablespoons fresh lemon juice

3 tablespoons cornstarch

½ cup water

FOR THE SHORTBREAD TOPPING:

½ cup (1 stick) unsalted butter, softened

½ cup granulated sugar

1 egg yolk

¾ cup all-purpose flour

½ teaspoon baking powder

Pinch of salt

Instructions

Preheat oven to 350°F.

In a medium-size saucepan, combine water and port or wine. Add berries, sugar, cinnamon, and lemon juice. Stir to combine and bring to a boil over medium heat. Whisk together cornstarch and ½ cup water to make a slurry. Stir into berry mixture and boil to thicken. Remove berries from heat and pour into eight individual ramekins or a 9 x 9-inch glass baking dish.

While berries are cooling, cream together the unsalted butter, sugar, and egg yolk in the bowl of a stand mixer fitted with the paddle attachment. In a separate bowl, whisk together flour, baking powder, and salt. Add flour mixture to the creamed butter and sugar and mix to combine.

Crumble shortbread on top of berry mixture. Bake until shortbread is golden brown and berry mixture is bubbling, about 10 to 12 minutes. Serve with vanilla bean ice cream.

CHEF'S TIP

Shortbread can be made ahead of time and chilled in the refrigerator.

Chico Wagon Wheels

These are made with ice cream from Livingston, Montana's famous Wilcoxson's, an iconic creamery in the nearby town since 1912. Our favorite flavor is Moose Tracks, a creamy vanilla packed with peanut butter chocolate cups, but there isn't a flavor that wouldn't work well with this quick dessert. These ice cream sandwiches taste best when shared with friends poolside at the hot springs.

MAKES 2 DOZEN COOKIES (OR 1 DOZEN ICE CREAM SANDWICHES)

Ingredients

½ cup (1 stick) unsalted butter

¾ cup granulated sugar

¾ cup brown sugar

2 large eggs

1 teaspoon pure vanilla extract

2¼ cups all-purpose flour

1 teaspoon fine salt

¾ teaspoon baking soda

¾ teaspoon baking powder

2 cups semisweet chocolate chips

4 cups vanilla ice cream

Instructions

TO MAKE THE CHOCOLATE CHIP COOKIES:
Cream butter and sugars together in an electric mixer with the paddle attachment. Slowly add eggs and vanilla to the creamed mixture. Add flour, salt, baking soda, and baking powder and mix until just combined. Add chocolate chips and mix for 30 seconds.

Preheat oven to 375°F. Spray a baking sheet with cooking spray.

Using a large spoon, scoop 2 ounces of dough and mound onto the baking sheet, leaving 2 inches between each cookie. Bake for 10 to 12 minutes, rotating pan halfway through the baking time. Remove from the oven and let cookies cool on pan.

TO ASSEMBLE THE WAGON WHEELS:
After cookies have cooled, add a ¼-cup scoop of your choice of ice cream onto the bottom of one cookie. Add the second cookie to sandwich the ice cream together. Serve immediately or refreeze for a cool treat later. If serving from the freezer, allow to sit for 5 to 10 minutes to soften the cookie.

Chocolate Coconut Almond Tart

An old favorite in the dining room, this is always featured on the dessert cart. Inspired by the Almond Joy candy bar, it is a delectable combination of dark chocolate and coconut combined in a toasted almond crust.

SERVES 12

Ingredients

FOR THE CRUST:

1½ cups toasted almonds

¼ cup lightly packed brown sugar

4 tablespoons (½ stick) unsalted butter, melted

FOR THE FILLING:

½ cup Coco Lopez cream of coconut (often found in the beverage section of the market)

3 ounces white chocolate, chopped

¼ cup sour cream

4 tablespoons (½ stick) unsalted butter, cut into pieces, room temperature

1¼ cups lightly packed shredded sweetened coconut

FOR THE TOPPING:

¼ cup heavy whipping cream

3 tablespoons unsalted butter

2 tablespoons light corn syrup

4 ounces bittersweet chocolate, chopped

2 ounces white chocolate, chopped and melted in double boiler

Instructions

TO MAKE THE CRUST:

Preheat oven to 350°F. Coarsely chop almonds in a food processor or blender. Add sugar and melted butter. Process the mixture until the texture is fine. Using plastic wrap as an aid, press mixture into the bottom and along the sides of a 9-inch tart pan with a removable bottom. Bake for 10 minutes. Remove the pan from the oven and let crust cool.

TO MAKE THE FILLING:

Bring coconut cream to a boil in a heavy saucepan. Reduce heat to low. Add white chocolate and stir until melted. Pour mixture into a medium bowl. Whisk in sour cream. Add butter and whisk until it melts into the batter and batter is a smooth consistency. Stir in shredded coconut. Chill until filling is very cold, but not set, about 1 hour. Spoon filling into crust and smooth the top. Chill until set.

TO MAKE THE TOPPING:

In a heavy saucepan, combine whipping cream, butter, and corn syrup and bring to a low boil, stirring frequently. Reduce heat to low. Add bittersweet chocolate and stir until melted. Pour over tart, covering filling. Spread topping with the back of a spoon to cover evenly. Spoon melted white chocolate into a pastry bag fitted with small tip. Pipe in parallel vertical lines over topping, spacing evenly. With a skewer or toothpick, drag the lines to form a decorative pattern in the dark chocolate. Chill and serve.

Montana Mud Pie ❂

Locally made Wilcoxson's ice cream is the star of this "pie." Any combination of ice cream will work. You can buy Wilcoxson's in Montana, Wyoming, and Idaho, as well as in Yellowstone National Park. Substitute your favorite flavors for each of the layers in this recipe. As simple as this no-bake recipe may appear, it still takes patience. Follow the freezing times for the best results. Make ahead if possible; the ice cream will keep in this form for up to a month without freezer burn.

SERVES 8–10

Ingredients

4 cups crushed chocolate cream-filled chocolate cookies (e.g., Oreos), divided

5 tablespoons unsalted butter, melted

3 cups coffee ice cream, slightly softened

1 cup crushed toffee

3 cups vanilla ice cream, slightly softened

1½ cups heavy whipping cream

1 pound semisweet chocolate squares

Instructions

TO MAKE THE CRUST:

Lightly spray a 10-inch pie plate (preferably glass) with cooking spray. (A 10-inch springform pan with removable bottom will be fine, too.) Combine 3 cups of crushed cookie crumbs with the melted butter and press into bottom and sides of the pie plate to form the crust. Place in the freezer until firm, at least 1 hour.

TO MAKE THE FILLING:

Create your first layer by placing the slightly soft coffee ice cream into a mixer fitted with a dough hook and mixing until smooth, but not runny. Or mix by hand until the ice cream is the consistency of a very thick milkshake.

TO ASSEMBLE THE PIE:

Remove crust from freezer and spread coffee ice cream onto the crust. Combine remaining 1 cup cookie crumbs with the crushed toffee. Reserve a handful for later and spread remaining mixture on top of the coffee ice cream. Place pie back into the freezer until very firm, at least 1 hour. Repeat the process with vanilla ice cream and place pie back into freezer again until very firm, at least 1 hour.

TO PREPARE THE CHOCOLATE GANACHE TOPPING:

Heat the heavy cream until just boiling and add semisweet chocolate. Remove from heat. Let stand for 2 minutes, then stir until smooth. Take pie from freezer and spread ganache over ice cream. Sprinkle the reserved handful of cookie and toffee mixture around the rim of the pie. Place pie into freezer for 2 hours before serving. Remove pie from freezer 10 minutes before slicing to serve.

Sour Cherry Pie

Montana's Nanking cherry season is a fleeting ten days in July, if you're lucky. The bushy trees that bear the small sour cherries don't always fruit, but when they do, it's a sprint to harvest these delicate-skinned jewels. They grow abundantly, but are not available commercially since they have a short shelf life and thin skin. Substitute Flathead (Lambert variety) cherries if sours aren't available.

SERVES 8

Ingredients

FOR THE CRUST:

6 ounces cream cheese, room temperature

½ pound (2 sticks) unsalted butter

2½ cups all-purpose flour

¼ cup milk (to brush on top crust)

FOR THE FILLING:

3 pounds Nanking cherries, pitted (or 2 pounds Flathead cherries)

1 cup plus 1 tablespoon granulated sugar, divided

¼ teaspoon salt

¼ cup cornstarch

1 teaspoon lemon zest (or 2 tablespoons lemon zest if using Flathead cherries)

1 tablespoon lemon juice (or 2 tablespoons lemon juice if using Flathead cherries)

1 teaspoon pure vanilla extract

1 tablespoon whole milk

Instructions

TO PREPARE THE CRUST:

In a mixing bowl, cream the cheese and butter until blended, then add the flour all at once. Mix until a dough ball forms. Divide into two balls, flatten, and wrap in plastic wrap. Place in the refrigerator until chilled, about 45 minutes to 1 hour.

TO PREPARE THE FILLING:

Gently mix cherries, sugar, salt, cornstarch, lemon zest and juice, vanilla, and milk in a bowl.

TO ASSEMBLE AND BAKE:

Preheat oven to 350°F. Remove one dough round from the refrigerator and roll into an 11-inch-diameter circle on a floured surface. Carefully fit into a 9-inch glass pie pan. Moisten edges of bottom crust with water. Fill crust with prepared cherry mixture.

Remove remaining dough round from the refrigerator, place on a lightly floured surface, and roll into an 11-inch-diameter circle. Place over top of the filling. Trim edges and gently tuck the top crust under the bottom crust. With your fingers, pinch a decorative edge all the way around the crust. Slice a few small vent holes in the top crust with a sharp knife, being careful not to cut through to the bottom crust. Brush top crust with milk, sprinkle remaining sugar over the crust, and place pie pan on a baking sheet to catch drippings.

Bake pie until filling is bubbling and crust is golden brown, about 1 hour, covering edges with a foil collar if browning too quickly. Transfer pie to a wire rack and cool completely. Cut into wedges and serve with vanilla ice cream.

Chico Carrot Cake

with Cream Cheese Mascarpone Frosting

It's humorous that carrot cake is often perceived as the "healthy" dessert. Just between friends, the carrots don't cancel out the calories. For a Chico twist we add mascarpone cheese to the frosting for a richer flavor to this dense cake.

SERVES 12 (MAKES 3 CUPS FROSTING)

Ingredients

FOR THE CAKE:

4 eggs

1½ cups granulated sugar

½ cup vegetable oil

2 cups all-purpose flour

1½ teaspoons ground cinnamon

½ teaspoon baking soda

½ teaspoon salt

2 cups shredded carrots, finely grated

1 cup finely chopped walnuts

FOR THE CREAM CHEESE MASCARPONE FROSTING:

½ cup (1 stick) unsalted butter

8 ounces softened cream cheese, room temperature

8 ounces mascarpone cheese, room temperature

3 cups sifted powdered sugar

1 tablespoon orange zest

¼ teaspoon salt

¾ cup finely chopped walnuts (optional)

Instructions

TO PREPARE THE CAKE:

Preheat oven to 350°F. Grease and flour two 9-inch round cake pans.

Whip the eggs and sugar for about 5 minutes, or until the mixture is very thick and pale yellow. Slowly add the oil and whip until combined.

Sift the flour, cinnamon, baking soda, and salt together and whisk to combine. Add to the egg batter and mix until well combined, scraping the sides and bottom of the bowl with a rubber spatula periodically. Fold in carrots and walnuts; dough will be thick and dense. Divide and spread the batter into the prepared pans and bake until the centers of the cakes spring back when touched with a finger, about 45 to 50 minutes. Cool for 5 minutes on a wire rack; turn cakes out of pans and allow to cool completely.

TO PREPARE THE FROSTING:

In an electric mixer on medium speed or by hand, beat the butter, cream cheese, and mascarpone cheese, scraping the sides and bottom of the bowl with a rubber spatula periodically, until well blended. Add the powdered sugar, zest, and salt; mix for 60 seconds more. Do not overmix or the frosting will not spread easily.

TO ASSEMBLE:

When cakes are cool, place one layer on a serving plate and spread a layer of frosting over the top. Place remaining cake on top for a simple two-layer cake. For a more elaborate presentation, slice each whole cake crosswise into two layers, making a total of four layers of cake. Place the bottom layer on a flat serving platter and spread a thin layer of frosting across the surface. Top with second layer and frost, repeating this process with the third layer, and finally adding the fourth layer on top of that.

Frost the top and sides of the entire cake. Press walnuts around the sides if desired. Serve chilled.

Grand Marnier Crème Brûlée ☕

The warmth of an after-dinner drink is combined with the smooth, creamy delicacy of crème brûlée in this traditional dessert.

SERVES 6

Ingredients

2 cups heavy whipping cream

⅓ cup granulated sugar

5 egg yolks, room temperature

½ tablespoon pure vanilla extract

¼ cup Grand Marnier, brandy, or other liqueur

6 teaspoons granulated sugar

Instructions

Preheat oven to 325°F. Heat the cream and sugar in a heavy saucepan until just boiling. Slowly pour in the egg yolks while whisking. Add the vanilla and the Grand Marnier. Pour into six ramekins or small, oven-safe bowls. Place in a 9 x 13-inch baking dish and fill with a hot water bath three-quarters of the way up the outside of the bowls. Bake for about 40 minutes, or until set; the brûlée should not jiggle in the center.

Remove from oven and let cool in the water bath. Refrigerate for at least 2 hours or up to 2 days covered with plastic wrap.

When ready to serve, sprinkle a teaspoon of sugar on top of each custard. With a small, handheld butane torch, caramelize the sugar until dark brown and bubbly. The result is a hot, delicate crust over a cool, creamy middle. (Handheld butane torches are available at most cooking shops.)

You can also caramelize the sugar in the oven by placing the custards under the broiler and watching carefully until the sugar is dark brown and bubbly, approximately 8 to 10 minutes; this will heat the bowl completely, resulting in a "soupy" texture and a crackly sugar layer.

Orange Blossom Brownies

The addition of orange zest in this recipe gives these decadent chocolate brownies a delicate balance of flavor that makes them appropriate at the most formal table or at a backyard barbecue.

SERVES 12

Ingredients

¼ cup butter, for greasing the pan

FOR THE BROWNIES:

6 eggs

1 cup canola oil

1 cup cocoa powder

3 cups granulated sugar

2 cups all-purpose flour, sifted

1 teaspoon salt

2 teaspoons pure vanilla extract

2 tablespoons freshly grated orange zest

½ cup chopped walnuts or pecans (optional)

FOR THE FROSTING:

4 cups powdered sugar

4 heaping tablespoons cocoa

½ cup evaporated milk

4 tablespoons (½ stick) unsalted butter, softened

1 teaspoon pure vanilla extract

Instructions

TO MAKE THE BROWNIES:

Preheat oven to 350°F. Grease two 8 x 8-inch baking dishes or one 9 x 13-inch baking pan.

In an electric mixer, beat eggs and oil. In a separate bowl, combine cocoa powder, sugar, flour, and salt. Stir until just combined.

Add vanilla, orange zest, and nuts if using to the egg mixture. Mix gently, only until just combined. Turn batter into pan(s) and bake for 40 to 45 minutes. Do not overbake. Leave in pan(s) to cool. Can be frosted or served plain.

TO MAKE THE FROSTING:

Combine all ingredients and mix on low speed until smooth, adding extra milk if necessary to make the icing more spreadable. When brownies are cool, spread the frosting, slice into squares, and serve.

Black Truffle Chocolate Tart
with Port-Infused Flathead Cherries

Rich. Decadent. Chocolate. Enough said.

SERVES 10–12

Ingredients

FOR THE TART DOUGH:

1½ cups all-purpose flour

1 teaspoon salt

¼ cup granulated sugar

½ cup (1 stick) unsalted butter, chilled

1 large egg, beaten

FOR THE GANACHE:

8 ounces semisweet dark chocolate

6 tablespoons unsalted butter

2 cups heavy cream

2 egg yolks

2 teaspoons black truffle oil

FOR THE PORT-INFUSED CHERRIES:

⅓ cup granulated sugar

1½ cups port wine

¾ cup pitted Flathead (Lambert variety) cherries (substitute raspberries if cherries are unavailable)

Instructions

TO PREPARE THE TART DOUGH:

Sift the flour, salt, and sugar into a mixing bowl. Cut the butter into small cubes. Rub it into the flour, using fingertips or a fork, until the mixture looks like fine bread crumbs. Make a well in the center and add egg. Mix by hand or with a fork to form a soft dough. Turn dough out onto a lightly floured surface, kneading gently until it is smooth and well combined. Wrap in plastic and chill for at least 30 minutes.

TO MAKE THE GANACHE:

Place chocolate and butter in a mixing bowl. In a saucepan, bring the cream to a boil. Pour hot cream over chocolate and butter. Let sit for 5 minutes. Add egg yolks and truffle oil. Mix with a rubber spatula until smooth, glossy, and well combined.

TO MAKE THE PORT-INFUSED CHERRIES:

In a small saucepan, combine sugar, port, and cherries. Simmer until sauce coats the back of a spoon. Refrigerate until ready for use.

TO ASSEMBLE:

Preheat oven to 350°F. Roll out chilled dough on a lightly floured surface to ¼ inch thickness and place in a 10-inch tart pan. Place parchment paper on dough. Weight with beans and bake until golden brown, about 12 to 15 minutes. This creates a shell for the ganache. Remove the crust from the oven and set aside to cool. When cool, pour ganache into the tart shell. Refrigerate for at least 2 hours or overnight. Slice and serve with port cherries.

Dulce de Leche Walnut Cake

This layer cake's homey appearance belies the many steps it takes to create the unforgettable ooey-gooey goodness and crunch that seem to embody the autumn season. Each step is well worth the end result, even just to impress guests who are lucky enough to sample a slice. It's the ideal finish for a holiday feast. To achieve the tall, layered effect, this recipe calls for four nine-inch round cakes, essentially a double batch, meaning this recipe should be made twice. For best results, with the four-cake version, make this recipe in two separate preparations; otherwise the batter won't fit in a standard home mixer and the frostings will not set right. Also, only bake two cakes at a time to ensure they cook evenly in the oven.

SERVES 12 (MAKES TWO CAKES)

Ingredients

FOR THE CANDIED WALNUTS:

6 tablespoons unsalted butter

2 cups walnut halves

½ cup packed light brown sugar

¼ teaspoon cinnamon

¼ teaspoon nutmeg

FOR THE CINNAMON BUTTER CAKE:

2 cups cake flour (not self-rising)

1 cup all-purpose flour

1 tablespoon baking powder

1 teaspoon salt

1 cup (2 sticks) unsalted butter, room temperature, plus more for greasing pans

1¾ cups granulated sugar

4 large eggs

2 teaspoons pure vanilla extract

1¼ cups whole milk

½ cup walnuts, finely chopped (optional)

FOR THE DULCE DE LECHE:

2 cups whole milk

1½ cups granulated sugar

¼ teaspoon baking soda

½ teaspoon pure vanilla extract

FOR THE CREAM CHEESE FROSTING:

One batch cream cheese mascarpone frosting, prepared in advance (recipe page 153), or two batches if you are planning the four-cake version.

Instructions

TO MAKE THE CANDIED WALNUTS:

Melt the butter in a large skillet over medium-high heat. Add the walnuts and cook, stirring, until golden brown and toasted, 3 minutes. Add the sugar and cook, stirring, for 2 minutes. Add the spices and stir to coat. Transfer to a piece of waxed paper to cool. The walnuts can be stored in an airtight container for up to 2 weeks.

TO MAKE THE CAKE:

Preheat oven to 350°F. Butter two 9-inch round cake pans and line the bottoms with parchment paper. Butter the parchment and dust with flour, tapping out excess; set aside. Into a medium bowl, sift together flours, baking powder, and salt; set aside.

In the bowl of an electric mixer fitted with the paddle attachment, beat the butter and sugar until light and fluffy, 3 to 4 minutes, scraping down the sides of the bowl as needed. Beat in eggs, one at a time, then beat in vanilla. With the mixer on low speed, add the flour mixture in three parts, alternating with the milk and beginning and ending with the flour; beat until combined after each addition. If using walnuts, add with the third alternation.

Divide batter among the prepared pans and smooth with an offset spatula. Bake, rotating the pans halfway through, until cakes are golden brown and a cake tester inserted into the center comes out clean, 30 to 35 minutes. Transfer pans to a wire rack to cool for 20 minutes. Invert cakes onto the rack; peel off the parchment. Re-invert cakes and let them cool completely, top-sides up. If you are making the four-cake layered version, you will make this recipe twice.

TO MAKE THE DULCE DE LECHE:

Combine milk, sugar, and baking soda in a heavy saucepan. Bring to a boil over medium heat without stirring. As mixture approaches a boil, it will foam up. Quickly remove it from the heat before it boils over; stir.

Turn stove to low and set the pan back on the heat, cooking slowly and stirring frequently with a wooden spoon for about 45 to 60 minutes. The mixture will gradually thicken and caramelize. When the mixture thickens to a rich brown sauce, remove from the stove and stir in the vanilla. Cool to room temperature.

TO ASSEMBLE:

Bring frosting to room temperature. Turn first cake over onto a serving dish or cake stand, smooth-side up and, using a metal frosting spatula, spread an even, thin layer over the surface. Place second cake on top of the frosted layer, flat-side up, and spread another smooth coating of frosting. Repeat with remaining two layers. Finish by ladling dulce de leche sauce over the top of all four layers and top with candied walnuts. The cake can stand at room temperature to impress your guests for several hours before dessert.

S'mores Campfire Bars

A sophisticated twist on the camping favorite, this version can be sliced and served on your best china or skewered and roasted over the fire. The homemade marshmallows are what really add a delicious special touch.

SERVES 12–24 (MAKES 24 INDIVIDUAL MARSHMALLOWS)

Ingredients

FOR THE MARSHMALLOWS:

Cooking spray

1 cup granulated sugar

½ cup light corn syrup

¾ cup cold water (divided)

4½ teaspoons (2 packages) powdered unflavored gelatin

2 teaspoons pure vanilla extract

2 cups powdered sugar

FOR THE CHOCOLATE GRAHAM COOKIE BARS:

Cooking spray

1½ cups all-purpose flour

1 cup graham flour (such as Bob's Red Mill brand; regular whole wheat flour can be substituted)

1 teaspoon baking soda

1 teaspoon baking powder

1 teaspoon salt

1 cup (2 sticks) unsalted butter

2 cups granulated sugar, divided

¾ cup firmly packed brown sugar

3 large eggs, room temperature

1 teaspoon pure vanilla extract

2 cups chopped high-quality semisweet chocolate

Instructions

TO MAKE THE MARSHMALLOWS:

Prepare a 9 x 13-inch baking pan with a light coat of cooking spray. Line the bottom of the pan with parchment paper, allowing for a 2-inch overhang on the long ends of the pan. Lightly coat the parchment with more cooking spray and set aside.

In a heavy saucepan, combine granulated sugar and corn syrup with ¼ cup cold water. Over medium-high heat, bring the mixture to a boil, stirring constantly to dissolve the sugar. As soon as the syrup mixture reaches a boil, stop stirring and place a candy thermometer into the pan. If it begins to foam, reduce heat slightly and stir. Continue cooking, stirring occasionally until the thermometer reads 240°F (soft ball stage). Remove the syrup from heat and pour it into the bowl of a stand mixer fitted with a whisk attachment. Let cool until it reaches 210°F.

While the syrup cools, place the remaining ½ cup cold water into a small bowl. Sprinkle the gelatin on top of the water, allowing it to soften, approximately 2 minutes. Add vanilla to the softened gelatin, stirring thoroughly. Combine the gelatin with the cooled sugar syrup.

On high speed, beat the syrup and gelatin until it is white and creamy, thick enough to hold a medium peak, 12 to 15 minutes. Pour the mixture into the prepared pan, smoothing it with a spatula to ensure it is evenly spread. Place in the freezer for 30 minutes.

CHEF'S TIP

The marshmallow slab can easily be cut into squares to make individual marshmallows that will elevate a cup of hot cocoa or the traditional campfire s'mores treat. To cut marshmallows into 2-inch pieces, lightly coat the blade of a large knife with cooking spray and dust with powdered sugar to prevent sticking. Toss marshmallow squares in powdered sugar until evenly coated. Marshmallows can be stored, layered between sheets of wax paper or parchment in an airtight container in a dry place at cool room temperature, for 1 month.

Prepare a cutting board by dusting the surface evenly with 1 cup powdered sugar. Remove marshmallow pan from freezer. Using the overhanging parchment sides, lift the slab of marshmallow and overturn it onto the sugared board. Thoroughly coat all surfaces of the marshmallow with powdered sugar, using the additional cup as needed. Set aside while making cookie bars.

TO MAKE THE CHOCOLATE GRAHAM COOKIE BARS:

Preheat oven to 375°F. Lightly coat a 9 x 13-inch baking pan with cooking spray. Sift flours, baking soda, baking powder, and salt into a bowl and set aside.

In a stand mixer fitted with the paddle attachment, cream butter, 1 cup of the granulated sugar, and brown sugar on medium speed until the texture is light and smooth. Add the eggs, one at a time, blending between additions until each is incorporated well. Add vanilla extract, then on low speed mix in the sifted dry ingredients, scraping down the bowl as needed to blend evenly.

Using a rubber spatula, spread the dough evenly into the pan. Bake for 20 to 25 minutes, or until a toothpick inserted in the center comes out clean.

Meanwhile, melt 2 cups of chopped semisweet chocolate over a double boiler. Keep warm until the graham bar is done. Remove the pan from the oven and pour the chocolate evenly over the top of the baked bar, smoothing with a spatula. Bring the marshmallow slab out of storage and gently place it on top of the chocolate layer. Let cool until chocolate is firm.

When ready to serve, sprinkle the remaining 1 cup granulated sugar evenly over the marshmallow layer. Using a kitchen hand torch, caramelize the marshmallow until just golden and slightly melted. Slice into twelve rectangular plated "cake" servings, or cut into twenty-four 1-inch squares and serve on a skewer for the effect of the nostalgic campfire treat.

Red Velvet Beet Cake
with Chocolate Swiss Meringue Buttercream

The abundance of the Chico garden has no boundaries. Even the dessert cart overflows with the seasonal harvest. Here the high concentration of sugar and the gorgeous color of beets add a deeper flavor while creating this moister, denser version of a red velvet cake.

SERVES 10–12

Ingredients

FOR THE CAKE:

3 medium beets

¾ cup buttermilk

Juice of 1 large lemon

2 teaspoons white vinegar

1½ teaspoons pure vanilla extract

2 cups cake flour (sift before measuring)

3 tablespoons Dutch process cocoa powder

1⅛ teaspoons baking powder

1 teaspoon salt

½ teaspoon baking soda

¾ cup (1½ sticks) unsalted butter, plus more for greasing pan

1¼ cups granulated sugar

3 eggs

FOR THE FROSTING:

1¼ cups granulated sugar

5 large egg whites

1½ cups (3 sticks) unsalted butter, room temperature

9 ounces bittersweet chocolate, melted and cooled

Instructions

TO MAKE THE CAKE:

Preheat oven to 350°F.

Wash beets and wrap in aluminum foil. Bake until the tip of a knife slides easily into the largest beet, about 1 hour, 15 minutes. Cool until beets can be handled, then peel. (This may be done up to a day ahead.)

Butter two 9-inch round cake pans. Line the bottoms of the pans with parchment and butter again.

In a food processor, chop beets to pieces about the size of finely diced onions. Measure 1 cup and set aside (remaining beets can be reserved for another purpose). Return the cup of beets to the food processor and add buttermilk, lemon juice, vinegar, and vanilla; puree until smooth.

Sift together flour, cocoa, baking powder, salt, and baking soda. Set aside.

In the bowl of a stand mixer, beat butter until soft. Slowly add sugar and beat until creamy. Beat in eggs, one at a time, scraping down the sides of the bowl after each addition. Alternate adding flour mixture and beet mixture to creamed butter, beginning and ending with the dry ingredients, and beating for 10 seconds after each addition. Scrape down the bowl after each addition of wet ingredients.

Divide batter between prepared cake pans, smoothing the tops. Bake until a cake tester inserted in the center comes out clean, about 20 minutes. Remove pans from the oven and cool completely on a wire rack.

TO MAKE THE FROSTING:

Whisk together sugar and egg whites in a heat-safe bowl. Place over a pot of simmering water, making sure that the water isn't touching the bottom of the bowl. Whisk until the sugar is completely dissolved and the egg whites reach 145°F, about 5 minutes.

Remove from heat and pour into the bowl of a stand mixer fitted with a whisk attachment. Whisk on high speed until egg whites have cooled, about 7 to 10 minutes.

Change to the paddle attachment and beat on medium-high speed. Add the butter 2 tablespoons at a time until combined. (Do not add butter too quickly or mixture will separate.) Beat in cooled chocolate.

TO ASSEMBLE:

Remove one cake from its pan and peel away parchment. Place the flat side down on a serving platter. Spread 1 cup of the buttercream frosting onto cake, using a flat spatula to spread it evenly over the top. Remove the second cake from its pan and peel away parchment. Place the flat side down on top of the frosted layer. Finally, frost the whole cake liberally with remaining chocolate buttercream, covering the top and sides of cake.

AUTUMN GLAMPING PARTY

TURNING ONTO THE LONG COUNTY ROAD heading toward the resort—the Absaroka Mountains to the east, the gentle foothills on the west, and awesome Emigrant Peak directly ahead—there is a lovely moment of anticipation. We're almost there! Chico is just one more mile ahead!

The actual arrival is like taking a step back in time. The historic building, squeaky doors, and sparse lobby haven't changed much since the hotel opened in 1900. Paying homage to the heroic pioneers who settled in this wild country over a century ago is Cowboy Camp, where guests stay in a Conestoga wagon.

Nestled on the hillside above the bustle of the main property, Cowboy Camp is Chico's answer to "glamping," or glamorous camping. It's a replica of the overland wagons that once traversed the United States during westward expansion. This version is a bit more deluxe than in the old days. Fully outfitted with a plush king-size bed, a bathhouse, and a private fireside lounge area, it's the ideal spot to catch the sunset and enjoy a romantic dinner for two. As the sky fades to twilight, popping the cork on a fine bottle of wine and sharing a light meal alfresco offers the chance to slow down. Away from the crowds, savor the sounds of the grasshoppers in the sage, the quiet of the valley, and the essence of stopping time.

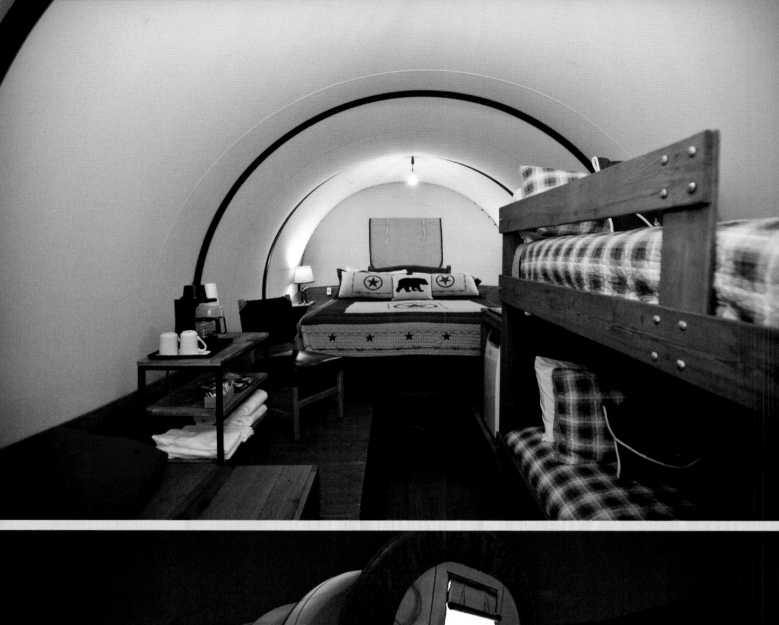

Wine and Spirits

CHICO'S WINE LIST WAS CRAFTED TO COMPLEMENT its classic cuisine as well as to appeal to the diverse clientele who walks through Chico's doors. From banker to rancher, from Europe to Livingston, there was a need to satisfy the palate of almost every guest. Our goal is to offer an approachable, affordable, and extensive collection of wines. We want our guests to be as comfortable selecting wine as they are ordering from our menu; at Chico that means quality and diversity. The idea is to be able to find easy-drinking favorites along with that aging Bordeaux or California cult classic tucked away for just the right customer.

Our list represents a wide variety of California and Northwest wines. The Italian and French offerings are extensive as well, laced with unusual jewels and hard-to-find vintages. The list also features larger-format bottles, from magnums of Silver Oak, Opus One, and Ornellaia to multi-bottle verticals of Beringer Private Reserve Cabernet, Italian Brunellos, and progressive years of Sassicaia. A further complement to the cuisine is the breadth of the champagne and dessert wine collection.

The restaurant has received *Wine Spectator* magazine's recognition since 1999. Chico wine cellar features more than 3,000 bottles of an extensive selection, garnering the Exclusive Award of Excellence recently and rendering Chico one of only two restaurants in the state of Montana to be recognized with the award. But more than acclaim, we've cultivated a loyal clientele who savors our program of food and wine. Careful planning and extensive staff training are all part of our wine program. Whether you select a familiar label or feel like trying something adventurous, our crew can pair wines to match your personal taste and meal.

Always inclusive of anything fun, the cocktail culture in the historic Lounge and Saloon offers a mixologist's interpretation of living in Montana. These concoctions represent the fresh and local philosophy that is embodied in the food, incorporating everything from honey harvested on our property to the spirits of micro-distillers in Bozeman, Helena, Manhattan, and Ennis. Cheers!

Montana-Moscow Mule

Ingredients

1½ ounces Dry Hills
Distillery's Hollowtop
Potato Vodka (Manhattan,
Montana)

¾ ounce fresh lime juice

4 ounces Cock and Bull
Ginger Beer

Instructions

Pour over ice in a chilled copper mug. Top off with Ginger Beer
and serve with a lime wedge.

Tumbleweed

Ingredients

1½ ounces Gulch Distillers'
Guardian Gin (Helena,
Montana)

½ ounce Chico honey
infused with Boulder
River Currant pu'erh tea
(Tumblewood Teas from
Big Timber, Montana)

½ ounce Dubonnet

½ ounce fresh lime juice

Instructions

Serve on the rocks with a Bordeaux cherry.

Ginger-Honey Old Fashioned

Ingredients

2 ounces Maker's Mark Bourbon

⅛ ounce ginger-infused honey

2–3 dashes of orange bitters

Grated cinnamon

Instructions

Ice and stir, then garnish with grated cinnamon and an expressed orange twist. For more aromatics and flair, create a "boat" with the orange and fill with a little Everclear, then ignite. Grate more cinnamon over the flame to set sparks flying.

Hot Rum Cider

Ingredients

2 ounces Bozeman Spirits Distillery's Prairie Schooner Spiced Rum

Hot apple cider

1 apple slice

1 orange twist

Instructions

Serve warm in a copper mug.

Chokecherry Blast

Ingredients

1½ ounces wild chokecherry–infused vodka

½ ounce fresh lemon juice

Club soda

Instructions

Serve over a tall glass of ice with a lemon wedge.

Zen Martini

Ingredients

Fresh muddled cucumber

1½ ounces Hendrick's Gin

½ ounce Pearls of Simplicity Sake

½ ounce simple syrup infused with fresh Chico garden mint

½ ounce fresh lemon juice

Instructions

Shake, strain, and serve "up" in a stemmed martini glass with a cucumber wheel.

WINTER WAGON RIDE AND BARN PARTY

AFTER A BRISK TROT ON THE COUNTY ROAD with two pretty Percherons pulling the Rockin' HK wagon, the warmth of the barn offers a cozy welcome. Set with a balance between rugged and refined, a dining table is tucked in between the horse manger and the tack room, warmed by outdoor heaters and a collection of friends in flannel and fleece.

The sun sets early during these winter months, and evenings turn toward the joy of a shared meal and a heartfelt toast. The menu may be plain, but it is succulent: an ample cheese and charcuterie board with Heirloom Bread, a brightly dressed green salad and a grilled steak with Hay Butter (just to prove that hay is not only for horses!), and a red velvet cake made from garden beets.

Inside, the barn glows warm with party lights strung from the rafters and lantern light on the tables. The saddle leather, rough wood, and modest decor creates a humble atmosphere to offset the elegant table. There is a sense of nostalgia in this building—in all barns most likely—a reminder of a simpler era. Settling in to this unlikely dining room is to embrace the essence of gathering to appreciate good things and good people.

In the Kitchen

EVERY COOK HAS A LARDER OR A PANTRY filled with staples that serve as the foundation for good food. There's no magic, just the basics of good cooking—excellent ingredients prepared with care. Many of the recipes in this book are elaborate and take some commitment. We try not to cut corners at Chico, preparing all of our stocks in-house and minimizing food waste by incorporating it into other dishes. The time-consuming techniques and sauces are what create the layers of flavor, texture, and taste that make each bite special. As a home cook it's not easy to invest so much effort to make one meal. We have tried to simplify the recipes for home cooking. On the other hand, executive chef Dave Wells asserts that if you can't make the time to cook from scratch, then it's probably not worth cooking at all. To that end, in this chapter you'll find essential sauces and stocks, additional details that add more depth to each dish, and some brief explanations of techniques to elevate your culinary skills. These are all elements of specific recipes, but they are also versatile components that can be added to your own concoctions and flavor pairings. This is by no means an end-all resource, but meant to offer building blocks for home cooks.

Beef Stock

MAKES 6 QUARTS

Ingredients

5 pounds beef bones (also called soup bones)

5 ounces tomato paste

4 large carrots, peeled and rough chopped

1 head celery, rough chopped

2 large white onions, rough chopped

1 bunch parsley or stems, rough chopped

3 bay leaves

1 tablespoon black peppercorns

2 tablespoons kosher salt

1 cup red wine

Instructions

Preheat oven to 400°F. Roast bones on a baking sheet until partially brown, about 20 to 25 minutes. Thin tomato paste with a little water and brush on bones.

Continue to roast until bones are dark brown but not burnt, about 45 minutes. Place bones and remaining ingredients in a large stockpot. Fill with cold water just over the top of the ingredients. Simmer over medium heat for 6 to 12 hours, then skim fat off the top and strain. Stock keeps up to 3 days in the refrigerator; if not used by then it should be frozen or discarded.

Chicken Stock

MAKES 6 QUARTS

Ingredients

1 whole chicken (3 pounds)

3 large carrots, peeled and rough chopped

6 stalks celery, rough chopped

2 large white onions, rough chopped

4 cloves garlic, rough chopped

1 bunch parsley or stems, rough chopped

3 bay leaves

2 tablespoons kosher salt

Instructions

Place chicken (including organs and neck) in a large stockpot; add remaining ingredients. Fill with cold water just over the top of the ingredients. Simmer over medium heat for 6 to 12 hours, then skim fat off the top and strain. Stock keeps up to 3 days in the refrigerator; if not used by then it should be frozen or discarded.

Duck Stock

MAKES 6 QUARTS

Ingredients

1 whole duck (at least 5 pounds)

3 large carrots, peeled and rough chopped

6 stalks celery, rough chopped

1 large yellow onion, rough chopped

4 cloves garlic, rough chopped

1 bunch parsley or stems, rough chopped

2 bay leaves

1 tablespoon black peppercorns

1 tablespoon kosher salt

Instructions

In a large stockpot, combine duck (including organs and neck) with remaining ingredients. Fill with cold water just over the top of the ingredients. Bring to a boil and let simmer for 6 to 8 hours, then skim fat off the top and strain. Stock keeps up to 3 days in the refrigerator; if not used by then it should be frozen or discarded.

Seafood Stock

MAKES 2 QUARTS

Ingredients

2 tablespoons vegetable oil

1 yellow onion, rough chopped

2 carrots, peeled and rough chopped

2 stalks celery, rough chopped

Uncooked reserved lobster and shrimp shells, well rinsed and drained

3 cups cold water, or enough to cover seafood shells

1 bay leaf

½ tablespoon black peppercorns

¼ teaspoon fennel seeds

1 teaspoon Pernod

Instructions

In a large stockpot, heat oil on medium high. Add onion, carrots, celery, and seafood shells. Cook until the onions are softened and the seafood shells are bright pink, stirring occasionally. Cover with cold water just over the top of the ingredients. Add bay leaf, peppercorns, fennel seeds, and Pernod. Allow the mixture to barely boil, then reduce heat to medium-low temperature and let simmer 20 minutes. Then strain into a clean pot, pressing down on the shells to extract all the liquid. Let cool uncovered, then refrigerate until ready to use. The stock will keep for one day in the refrigerator; if not used by then it should be frozen or discarded.

Compound and Infused Butters and Crostini
Garlic Butter

MAKES ½ POUND

Ingredients

1 cup (2 sticks) unsalted butter, softened

1 teaspoon dry mustard

1 teaspoon Worcestershire sauce

1 teaspoon minced garlic

1 teaspoon fresh thyme

Instructions

Mix all ingredients thoroughly with an electric mixer or by hand using a wooden spoon. While butter is soft, roll it into a 1 x 6-inch log in plastic wrap and refrigerate.

Hay Butter

Typically the regional grasses of Montana are dried and bundled into hay for agricultural use to feed horses and cattle throughout the year. Chef Dave Wells introduced this unique infusion of the barnyard ingredient into butter and usually pairs it with a rangier cut of beef, preferably grass-fed and from Montana, such as a flank steak (see Main Courses, page 131). The result is a subtle nutty, herbaceous layer of flavor that's unforgettable. Meat, poultry, or even vegetables can be rubbed in butter prior to grilling and then finished with a drizzle just before serving.

MAKES 1 POUND

Ingredients

2 cups (4 sticks) unsalted butter, cubed

1 ounce organic hay (about a handful), washed

Instructions

On low heat melt butter and hay together in a large, deep pan. Once melted, let the hay infuse the butter over the low heat for 1 hour. Remove from stovetop and drain through a fine-mesh sieve. Use what's needed for immediate service; the rest can be reserved for later. For small servings, pour the remaining butter into an ice cube tray and freeze; it will keep for 2 months.

Crostini

MAKES 1 LOAF

Ingredients

1 loaf Heirloom Bread (recipe page 43), cut in ½-inch-thick slices

¼ cup extra-virgin olive oil

Instructions

Preheat oven to 400°F. Brush bread slices with olive oil on both sides. Bake for 10 to 15 minutes in the oven; reserve until later or serve immediately.

Sauces and Salad Dressings
Chimichurri Sauce

MAKES 2 CUPS

Ingredients

¼ cup minced fresh oregano

1 cup minced fresh flat leaf parsley

1 cup minced fresh cilantro

½ cup red wine

¾ cup extra virgin olive oil

2 tablespoons minced shallots

½ teaspoon red pepper flakes

½ teaspoon salt

¼ teaspoon fresh ground pepper

Instructions

Combine all ingredients in a blender, or whisk by hand, until emulsified. The sauce can be used as a marinade for grilled vegetables, seafood, and meats. As a sauce, serve at room temperature to allow the herbaceous flavors to stand out.

Fresh Citrus Vinaigrette

MAKES 2 CUPS

Ingredients

1 grapefruit

1 orange

1 lemon

1 lime

1 teaspoon Dijon mustard

¼ cup extra-virgin olive oil

1 teaspoon granulated sugar

½ teaspoon salt

Instructions

Juice all fruits and combine with remaining ingredients in a blender, or whisk by hand, until emulsified. Chill.

Hollandaise Sauce

MAKES ABOUT 1 CUP

Ingredients

1 cup (2 sticks) plus 2 ablespoons unsalted butter

3 egg yolks, room temperature

2 tablespoons white wine

Juice of 1 lemon

1 teaspoon salt

½ teaspoon cayenne pepper

Instructions

To prepare clarified butter, melt butter over medium heat and skim foam off the top with a large spoon. Heat clarified butter to 95°F. In a separate saucepan, add egg yolks and white wine; whisk over medium heat until the mixture thickens (about 3 minutes). Remove mixture from heat and slowly drizzle the 95°F butter into the pan, constantly stirring. (The temperature of the butter is crucial; measure it with a thermometer.) Once all butter has been incorporated, add lemon juice, salt, and cayenne pepper while continuing to stir.

Moose Drool BBQ Sauce

MAKES 4 CUPS

Ingredients

1 yellow onion, finely diced

¼ cup garlic, minced

2 tablespoons unsalted butter

12 ounces Moose Drool brown ale

½ teaspoon crushed red pepper flakes

1½ teaspoons black pepper

1 tablespoon blackening (Cajun) spice

¾ cup apple cider vinegar

¼ cup molasses

1 cup brown sugar

1 tablespoon Worcestershire sauce

2 dashes Tabasco sauce

4 cups tomato sauce

Instructions

In a large stockpot, brown the onions and garlic in butter over medium heat for about 5 minutes. Deglaze with Moose Drool beer and reduce. Add red pepper flakes, black pepper, blackening spice, and vinegar; stir until liquid is reduced by ⅓. Add molasses, brown sugar, Worcestershire, Tabasco, and tomato sauce and bring to a boil. Reduce heat and let simmer for 1 hour. Make ahead if desired; sauce will keep in the refrigerator for 2 weeks.

Doughs and Crust

Pie Dough

SERVES 4

Ingredients

1¾ cups all-purpose flour

6 large egg yolks

Instructions

Pour flour onto a wooden cutting board or countertop and make a well in the center. Pour eggs into the center and, using fingers, begin stirring the eggs with the flour until it is all absorbed and forms a shaggy dough. Begin to knead the dough, pushing forward on the board until all the lumps are absorbed and the dough becomes silky smooth. Knead for 15 minutes, then wrap in plastic so it doesn't dry out and let rest for 30 minutes to an hour.

The dough can be made a day ahead, wrapped in plastic, and refrigerated; bring to room temperature before proceeding with a recipe.

Pie Crust

MAKES 1 DOUBLE CRUST

Ingredients

1 cup (2 sticks) unsalted butter, chilled

6 ounces cream cheese, chilled

2½ cups all-purpose flour

Instructions

Cut butter into cubes. Cream the cheese and butter with an electric mixer until blended. Add the flour all at once. Mix until a dough ball forms, then remove from bowl. Divide into two balls, flatten, and wrap in plastic wrap. Place in the refrigerator until chilled, about 45 minutes to 1 hour.

Preheat oven to 350°F. On a lightly floured surface, roll out one ball of dough until it is 11 inches in diameter and fit it into a pie pan. Add desired filling. Roll out the second ball and press over top of the pie, folding the top edge under and pressing to seal. Bake for 40 to 45 minutes until crust is golden brown.

Chipotle Remoulade for Burgers

MAKES 1½ CUPS

Ingredients

1 cup mayonnaise

½ cup diced dill pickle

1 chipotle pepper (canned in adobo sauce), diced

1 tablespoon apple cider vinegar

1 teaspoon minced roasted garlic

1 teaspoon granulated onion

1 teaspoon salt

2 tablespoons chopped fresh parsley

Instructions

Mix all ingredients thoroughly and chill until served.

Red Onion Marmalade

MAKES ABOUT 1 CUP

Ingredients

2 medium red onions, julienned

4 tablespoons (½ stick) unsalted butter

1 teaspoon kosher salt

3 tablespoons red wine

3 tablespoons balsamic vinegar

2 tablespoons brown sugar

½ teaspoon cayenne pepper

½ teaspoon cinnamon

Instructions

Sauté the onions with butter in a skillet over medium-high heat with the salt. Cook, stirring often, for about 10 to 12 minutes, or until the onions are golden. Add the wine and cook for 2 minutes, stirring constantly. Add the vinegar, sugar, cayenne, and cinnamon; cook for another minute. Remove from heat, cool, and serve.

Marmalade can be refrigerated in an airtight container for up to 1 week.

Roasted Garlic

MAKES 4 HEADS ROASTED GARLIC

Ingredients

4 large heads of garlic

¼ cup olive oil

Aluminum foil

Instructions

Preheat oven to 350°F. Cut the tops of the heads off and place each head on a piece of aluminum foil big enough to completely wrap around the garlic. Pour oil over the top of the garlic and wrap with foil, then place in an oven-safe dish and cook in the oven for around 45 minutes, or until garlic is very soft.

COOKING TECHNIQUES
Brining and Curing

Brining is the process of soaking vegetables, meat, or fish in a saltwater mixture to add moisture and flavor. You can even brine cheese (feta, for instance). The result is an extra dimension of flavor and assurance that your protein won't dry out when it's cooked. Brining vegetables is actually considered pickling. This method is implemented in the Pan-Roasted Chicken with Herbed Veloute Sauce (recipe page 113) and is the essential step in cooking unforgettable chicken.

The process of curing poultry, meats, and fish is an ancient preservation method. It's a method implemented frequently in the Chico kitchen (see the preparation for a confit duck leg in Duck Grand Marnier Two Ways, recipe page 121). Using either salt or sugar and a choice of seasoning, it's a method that enhances flavor and texture, though unlike brining you don't dissolve the salts and sugars in water. After curing, remember to rinse your meat or fish to clear the curing element from the flesh; this eliminates the chance that your dish will be excessively salty or sweet. Rinse and pat dry. Brining and curing are often first steps in smoking.

Smoking

An array of home smokers are available on the market. At Chico we use a large electric smoker with apple wood chips. Most of the recipes in this book offer an adaptation for a home barbecue grill, which is much simpler than it sounds at first. It only requires a thermometer on the grill and a little extra patience to experiment.

Hardwoods such as alder, apple, oak, and cherry—all sold commercially as chips—infuse fish, poultry, meats, and even cheese with a mild smokiness. Remember that a little wood goes a long way; 1 to 2 cups of soaked wood chips are sufficient for most home recipes. The more time ingredients remain in the "smoke," the stronger the flavor will be in the food, and finding the delicate balance of flavor takes finesse.

Smoked Trout

MAKES 2 POUNDS

Ingredients

FOR THE BRINE:

½ gallon water, room temperature

1 cup kosher salt

½ cup brown sugar

1 tablespoon mild yellow curry powder

1 whole cleaned fish or fillets

Instructions

Mix water, salt, sugar, and curry powder until thoroughly dissolved in a glass or ceramic container that is large enough to hold the fish you are smoking. Place fish in brine, submerging with the skin facing up. Place a large plate on top of fish to keep them underwater.

Refrigerate in brine for 1 hour. Remove fish from brine, lightly rinse in cold water, and pat dry. Place fish on lightly oiled baker's racks, with fillet meat spread open, skin-side down.

Smoke at 180°F following manufacturer's instructions for 1 hour. Fish are done when they flake easily with a fork or when the internal temperature reaches 140°F. Remove and let trout cool for 30 minutes. Wrap in foil and place in a resealable plastic bag to refrigerate until ready to serve.

Smoked Chèvre

MAKES 8 OUNCES

Ingredients

8 ounces chèvre (Bozeman's Amaltheia Dairy produces a sharp and creamy goat cheese)

Instructions

To smoke, spread chèvre evenly in a shallow dish, such as a cake pan. Don't spread it out too thin or it will dry out. Next, place a pan of ice under the chèvre pan and place in a smoker with apple wood chips at 180°F for 40 minutes.

Alternatively, if you don't own a home smoker, it's simple to turn a barbecue grill into a custom smoker within minutes. Soak apple wood chips (readily available at a good hardware store or cooking shop) for about an hour. Meanwhile, fire up the grill (yes, even if it's a propane grill), heating coals to 180°F. When the fire comes to the right temperature, place wood chips and cheese (with ice) onto the rack, close the lid, and smoke for 30 to 40 minutes. (The water-soaked wood chips can be placed in a pan and set on top of the grill; the cheese will nestle onto another sheet pan of ice next to the wood chips.) The process infuses the cheese with an earthy smokiness. With a rubber spatula, scrape the cheese into a jar and set aside until it's time to serve. After it is smoked, the cheese is a fantastic addition to most dishes, from salad to crackers.

Sous Vide

This method of pre-cooking proteins that are vacuum sealed in plastic and cooked slowly in water at a low temperature is a French technique that has become popular—mostly in restaurants—over the last fifteen years. In a commercial setting it's designed to ensure the exact preparation for the ingredient so that it can be served the same way every time. No more overcooked or undercooked steaks getting sent back to any kitchen. The sous vide method is easily replicated with a home appliance and is a worthy experiment.

In the Chico kitchen, the Mustards Pork Chop (recipe page 129) is marinated and prepared sous vide and then finished over an open flame.

High-Altitude Cooking and Baking

Normally anything made above 3,000 feet is considered high-altitude cooking. All the recipes in the book are regularly prepared at 5,300 feet; they have been tested at altitudes above 4,000 feet. If you live at 3,000 feet or below, then you can expect minor adjustments when preparing these dishes. Essentially you are converting to "low-altitude cooking," mostly when baking. Beyond water or sauces coming to a boil faster at lower altitude, the other recipes remain the same. There are no hard and fast rules for altitude adjustments in cooking, but here are some suggestions to make your recipes more accurate.

For cakes: The most appealing characteristic of a cake is its delicacy. Adjust the recipe by increasing the sugar by 1 to 2 tablespoons per cup and reducing the liquid by 2 tablespoons to compensate for less liquid evaporation at lower altitudes.

Next, reduce each teaspoon of baking powder by ¼ teaspoon. Finally, reduce each cup of liquid by 2 tablespoons. (This applies to the Chico Carrot Cake with Cream Cheese Marscapone Frosting and the Dulce de Leche Walnut Cake; recipes pages 153 and 161.)

For quick breads: Increase the sugar by 1 to 2 tablespoons per cup to compensate for less liquid evaporation at lower altitudes. Expect that cobblers and pies baked at an altitude lower than 3,000 feet may take 10 to 15 minutes less time to cook than suggested in these recipes. (This applies to the Orange Blossom Brownies and the Sour Cream Coffee Cake Muffins; recipes pages 157 and 14.)

CHICO

HOT SPRINGS RESORT

Happy Trails

Duncan Kippen

HAPPY TRAILS

CHICO IS THE KIND OF PLACE THAT OFFERS the comfort that comes with history, like the security of returning to your hometown after a long journey. There's a sense that it will always be here, just as you remembered it, unchanged and suspended in the stories and memories we've all made here.

Each person who visits this authentically western, genuinely funky, and beautifully remote resort only arrives as a stranger once. It's a place that has been here longer than all of us have lived on this earth, so it can't really be owned, it can only be shared. We hope that you will share it with us and others, again and again.

Happy trails, from the Chico Hot Springs family.

Resources

AMALTHEIA DAIRY
Since 2005, the goat farm has been making silky chèvre in Belgrade, Montana.
www.amaltheiadairy.com; (406) 388-0569

BARNEY CREEK LIVESTOCK
Grass-fed cattle raised in Paradise Valley with sustainable grazing practices that are good for the land and good for the animals.
No website; (406) 640-2956

BIG SKY BREWING CO.
Based in Missoula, Big Sky brews some of Montana's best-known beers, including Moose Drool and Trout Slayer.
www.bigskybrew.com; (406) 549-2777

GARDEN CITY FUNGI
Organically grown high quality gourmet mushrooms and a seasonal source for wild harvested morels and chanterelles near Missoula, Montana.
www.gardencityfungi.com; (406) 626-5757

KATABATIC BREWERY
Full-bodied craft beer brewed in Livingston, Montana.
www.katabaticbrewery; (406) 333-2855

MONTANA ROOTS
Aquaponically grown microgreen and sprouts grown in a greenhouse just steps away from the Yellowstone River near Livingston, Montana.
www.montanaroots.org; (406) 848-1428

MONTANA WAGYU COMPANY
Supplying Kobe beef and Kurobuta pork that are luxuriously marbled while also robustly textured, all from Belgrade, Montana.
www.montanawagyu; (406) 451-5513

TIMELESS SEEDS, INC.
America's only organic gourmet legume and grain producer is located in Montana's golden triangle in the north-central section of the state.
www.timelessfood.com; (406) 866-3340

TROUT CULTURE, INC.
Rainbow trout raised in the natural environment of Montana water, hand-fed organic food and hand-caught.
www.troutculture.com; (406) 763-6328

TUMBLEWOOD TEAS
Exotic flavors blended in Big Timber, Montana, and served hot in the Chico dining room.
www.tumblewoodteas.com; (406) 932-9641

WILCOXSON'S ICE CREAM
Serving Livingston, Montana's sweet treat throughout the state since 1912, the smooth, creamy concoctions are made from Montana dairy cow milk.
www.wilcoxsonsinc.com; (406) 222-2370

WOLF RIDGE LAMB AND WOOL CO.
Just down the road from Chico, 100 percent grass-fed lamb, raised as natural as possible (no sub-therapeutic antibiotics, grain, or growth hormones) created from the high-quality pastures where they graze in Paradise Valley.
www.wolfridgeicelandics.com; (406) 333-4031

YELLOWSTONE GRASS-FED BEEF
It's beef at its simplest, purest, and most delicious. It's 100 percent grass-fed, 100 percent grass-finished and free of hormones and antibiotics.
www.yellowstonegrassfedbeef.com; (406) 522-9421

Index

About the Author and Photographer

SEABRING DAVIS is a writer by profession and a cook by passion. She won the culinary High Plains Book Award in 2016 for the cookbook *A Taste of Montana* and is the author of several other books, including *A Montana Table: Recipes from Chico Hot Springs Resort*. She writes broadly about the things she loves: food, art, and interesting people. She has spent a lifetime at the keyboard of a computer, as a magazine editor, newspaper obituary reporter, activist, essayist, food blogger, and feature writer. But when the screen powers down, she can't wait to get in the kitchen, where creativity and beauty and nature's generosity come together in the best and most satisfying ways. She lives in Livingston, Montana, with her husband and two daughters.

LYNN DONALDSON-VERMILLION is a Livingston, Montana–based photojournalist whose appetite for adventure and thirst for travel have her roaming throughout the Rocky Mountains shooting and writing about Sugar Beet Festivals, Catholic Burgers, Wild Game Cook-Offs, and the absolute best places to eat pie. She is the founder and creative director of the Montana food and travel blog TheLastBestPlates.com, and you can find her stories and images in *National Geographic Traveler*, *Saveur*, TheFoodNetwork.com, *Travel + Leisure*, *Food & Wine*, *Sunset*, the *New York Times*, the *Wall Street Journal*, and many other national publications. Lynn is also a featured Instagrammer for Nat GeoTravel and has chronicled mermaid bars in Central Montana, taimen fishing in Mongolia, and morel hunting in the Absaroka-Beartooth Wilderness. Her weekly newspaper column, "The Last Best Plates," appears each Wednesday in the *Billings Gazette*, *Missoulian*, *Montana Standard*, *Helena Independent Record*, and *Ravalli Republic*. She shoots the "Dining Out" column, written by Seabring Davis, for *Big Sky Journal*. Donaldson-Vermillion has shot two additional cookbooks: *Open Range: Steaks, Chops and More from Big Sky Country* and *New Frontier Cooking: Recipes from Montana's Mustang Kitchen*. She and her adventurer husband are raising three spirited children who love eating everything from Southern barbecue and Bahamian conch to Mongolian Khorkhog. When not scouring the globe in search of appetizing stories, the Vermillion family can be found on the trails and streams surrounding Livingston.